A Guide on Jazz Piano, Composition and Arrangement Textbooks

Between 1933 & Today

TPAF

A Guide on Jazz Piano, Composition, and Arrangement Textbooks (English Edition)
~between 1933 and today~

Author & Editer：Koji Kawai, Akira Kawai
Copyright ©2020 by TPAF
ISBN: 9784906858361
TPAF
1-42-8-107 Minamiogikubo, Suginami-ku,Tokyo,167-0052,Japan
http://www.tpafart.com
media@tpafart.com

Introduction

This guide provides an introduction to 260 different jazz piano, composition and arrangement textbooks written between 1933 and today.

Though this may be hard to believe, there have been just as many, if not more jazz piano textbooks published in Japan as there have been in the U.S. Most notably, Eiichi Fujii, Yasutoshi Inamori, and Tomoyuki Hayashi have each authored over 100 jazz piano textbooks.

In a time when the internet didn't exist as it does today, I would search for textbooks by a few different means which included referring to ads in American Jazz magazines like DownBeat, ordering catalogs from secondhand stores in New York, or asking friends who had studied at the Berklee College of Music, and then purchase any new textbook that caught my attention. Of course, nowadays, there are many more publishers in general, and an abundance of books that are quite similar to one another, so I haven't been purchasing as many publications as I once did. At the same time, I have taken a kind of philological, archaeological interest in unearthing the authors and publication dates of some of the earliest written jazz piano textbooks, and I decided to include many of these elusive, out-of-print works in this guide.

I've also written about how I've personally worked with jazz piano manuals over the years through some of my own experiences, and noted where I had questions or doubts about the material or the way it was presented. I hope they can be of some use to aspiring students like yourself.

Furthermore, I have limited this guide to the textbooks which I actually purchased and played through. Although it really goes without saying, this is because it would be just as impossible a task to review a textbook without having played through it as it would be to critique a CD or album without having listened to it. Consequently, I believe there are a number of works, some of which are highly acclaimed by instructors and students, that are missing in this guide when looking at the textbooks included from the perspective of jazz piano instruction as a whole. In this regard, I must take this opportunity here to apologize. I hope to include these works in future revised editions.

The points to keep in mind in this document are as follows.

1. Book title, author name, publisher (publisher) name, publication year from left.

2. The publication date is shown from the oldest one.

3. Since jazz pianists are also composers, I have shown as much as possible the textbooks on composition and arrangement.

4. In a series of books, if the publication year of each book is different, the ones that are connected in terms of content are introduced together with the books with earlier publication years.

5. Books not published in the publication year were published in the estimated year.

6. I worked to show as many out-of-print books as possible.

7. When both the original and the Japanese translation are available, the original is given priority. Due to various reasons, such as difficulties in obtaining materials, some books are only Japanese translations.

In addition, I picked up recommendation books from the textbooks introduced in this book (P106).

It also describes the style of jazz piano learning on the Web (P107-108).

We look forward to receiving your honest opinions and comments regarding this document. Thank you very much.

Koji Kawai, Akira Kawai

Encounter with jazz piano textbooks

When I was in high school I was interested in jazz, and at that time the jazz world was a solo piano boom. Pianists such as Cecil Taylor, McCoy Tyner, Chick Corea, Keith Jarrett, Daller Brand, and Stanley Cowell have been releasing solo piano albums one after another. Meanwhile, I came to want to play jazz piano. But I didn't know how to play jazz piano. So, on the way home from school, I decided to go to a music store at Ochanomizu or Ginza in Tokyo and buy and play some jazz piano instruction books. However, there are few textbooks that are useful for jazz performances, and no jazz-like sound is produced when using any textbook. Because they were all "classical style" textbooks of jazz piano, like "ragtime", "boogie woogie" and "swing style". At that time, in addition to the solo piano boom, Miles Davis was playing electric-sound music. It was a time when fusion music was popular. In Japan, however, even a practical "modern jazz piano" textbook had not yet been published.

Nevertheless, the following two textbooks were helpful to some extent.

First,on the left, there is no introductory explanation of the Jazz piano techniqueVolume 2, Modern Jazz' (Masanobu Higurashi / Rhythm Echos: Not published in the year of publication) chord work, so it seems to be an intermediate level textbook. There are many examples of chord progression and substitute chords, but they were all too abrupt and difficult to understand. The right side of (Kaoru Iiyoshi/Zenon: Not published in the year of publication) is 'Introduction to jazz piano' (Even now, they are sometimes listed on Yahoo Auction.), and the author, Kaoru Iiyoshi, appeared on a music TV program by Yasushi AKUTAGAWA. So I knew his name. There's a lot of chorde work and ad-lib, but most of the chord is up to 7th. Adlib, The adlib was quite informative, including Bud Powell's Transcription (a copy phrase) (although this book is rarely seen recently). I knew most later that the former "Jazz Piano Technique" was written on pages 65-66, and the latter "Introduction to Jazz Piano" was written on page 32, with about 6 measures, but the chord work used in actual jazz performances was written. I didn't notice that at that time. In short, it was an era where information could not be disseminated and much could not be opened.

When I consulted with my high school music teacher (A graduate of the vocal department of a music college, he had students listen to Blebeck's Take Five records in class), He lent me 'impression of New York' (Dave Bluebeck/Toa Music: 1966: Left Figure). There were no adlibs, only themes, but I learned a lot about voicing block chrod.
In the case of Eb 7, does the left hand omit Root and play "G, D ♭ , F "? And ... But it was full of things I still couldn't understand.
Incidentally, although there is no table of contents for "Toki's Theme Toki's Theme" from "Impressions of Japan" as an appendix, it is listed in the first track (4P.) "Upstage Rumba" is a unique song written in a twelve-tone technique based on Latin rhythm. Brubeck expresses what he learned from Schoenberg.

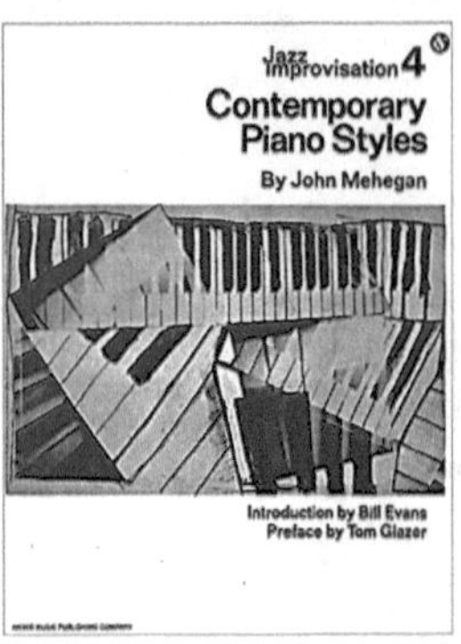

In the meantime, I learned about the existence of the Jazz Improvisation series by John Megan. There are up to four volumes, but volumes one and two have been published in Japanese translations, and volume one is the principle of sound and rhythm (chord symbols are classified into three categories: II—V, diatonic, and chromatic). Looking at the publicity of the other volume at the end of the book, the textbook titled "Jazz Improvisation Contemporary Piano Styles" (John Megan / AMSCO: 1965) Discovery, I thought, "Maybe this book!" For the fourth volume, a Japanese book was not yet published, so I purchased the original book (left figure).It was a very thick book, but when I played it, I heard a jazz sound. I was moved by this. The chord work was divided into A form and B form depending on the form, but I was absorbed in practicing. In about a few months, I was almost able to play.

In 1975, the author, Sadayasu FUJII, published a textbook called "JAZZ PIANO IMPROVOSATION 1~3" Sadayasu FUJII/Ritto Music: 1975) that copied the performances of pianists such as McCoy Tinner, Chick Korea, and Windong Kelly. (Left). After that, Sadayasu FUJII published practical jazz textbooks one after another such as 'jazz piano mode playing' (Rittmusic) 'the technique of improvisation practiced with the keys of a jazz piano 12' and (Litto Music). It can be said that the wall of the Jazz textbook was destroyed by Sadayasu FUJII, just as the Berlin wall was destroyed.

Just as the Berlin Wall collapsed, it can be said that the collapse of the jazz textbook in Japan was done by Sadayasu Fujii.

So why wasn't a practical jazz piano textbook published in Japan until then? I think there are several reasons for this. For one thing, because the essence of jazz is improvisation, it seems that there was a sense of resistance to using sound as a score like classical music. Furthermore, with classical music, even if the music system and overall picture are shown by the score, considerable training is required to play difficult songs. However, in the case of jazz, as long as you know the playing methodology, you can play even if you don't have any technique. Therefore, anyone who knows how to play jazz can play jazz (although it is not). Then it will be a problem as a professional musician. Therefore, he may have wanted to keep the performance method as secret as possible.

By the way, many jazz textbooks have been published since the late 70's when the Berlin Wall of jazz textbooks collapsed and after 1980, and in particular Eiichi Fujii, Yasutoshi Inamori and Tomoyuki Hayashi each issued about 100 textbooks. I guess. By the way, in the United States, there were several excellent books on jazz piano, such as the one introduced by John Megan. However, in the United States, as in Japan, many practical textbooks are issued after 1980.

In that respect, a large number of textbooks have been published. However, because of the large number of publications, you may be wondering what to buy.

In addition, since classical music has a fixed sound in the score, the overall picture of the target music is clear and the method can be easily squeezed. But because Jazz is improvised and jazz pianist is also a composer, it is difficult to present a textbook that will be a step to satisfy such a wide range of musical skills and backgrounds. The textbooks used also differ depending on the learner's musical background. "I have never played an instrument, but I like jazz and want to play the piano." For example, "I never played jazz, but I used to play a little classical piano." I've never played a guitar or trumpet etc

In other words, the textbook used differs depending on the learner's musical background.

Therefore, a recommendation book was introduced in p107 to help such diverse learners. I hope you find it helpful.

8. A Guide on Jazz Piano, Composition, and Arrangement Textbooks

A Guide on Jazz Piano, Composition, and Arrangement Textbooks

~between 1933 and today~

『Vincent Lopez Modern Piano Method Book I』 (Vincent Lopez /M M COLE PUBLISHING CO)1933

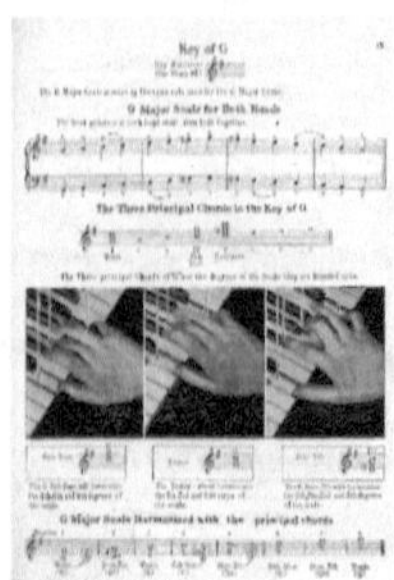

Gutenberg's letterpress technology has had a lot of impact on musicians.

Selling music became an important task for musicians to support their living base. Especially in the late 19th century, there were many music publishers in Timpan Alley near Broadway, New York. "Sheet Music" in Jazz must have been published mainly around this tympan array. That's why all the European composers, such as Debussy, Stravinsky and Rabel, created jazz-inspired work, which was what sparked jazz's global reach. However, as the phonograph progressed and the record culture flourished, music publishers declined. Most of today's music publishers are right business organizations called "master production" and "management of publishing rights".

Although the introduction has been lengthened, Jazz's "Sheet Music" will be one of the oldest in the jazz piano textbooks, even though it is thriving on the Timpan Array. The author, Vincent Lopez, was a pianist and band leader, founding his orchestra in 1917, gaining popularity through radio programming in 1921, and was the most popular band leader in the United States until the 1940s. His orchestra included Arty Shaw, Tommy Dorsey and Glen Miller.

By the way, this jazz piano textbook has up to four volumes in total, and this book is the first volume. Beginning with the basic principles of music, such as starting with the explanation of music staff, it explains what position the piano keys correspond to in the staff, and explains fingering with pictures of hands. From P13, explanation of the positioning of the main triad on the left and right, and the inverted form. P18 shows the rhythm pattern of the actual performance using "Old Black Joe" as an example. From P19 to P63, the same description is given for each key. Explain the scale to be used, the chord to be used with finger rings with photos, positioning of both hands, rhythm pattern, and actual music examples (Mass in the Cold Ground for G key, Gypsy lament for Em key) Etc.). In the last P64, 36 patterns of the left hand with the Major, Minor, and Seventh chords (played since the lag time, alternately root and triad, 5th and triad alternately jump to "Zun Cha") are posted. ing. It can be said to be the basics of jazz piano in the swing era, and also the basics of piano practice.

『Dance Arranging』 (Paul Weirick/Witmrk Educational Publications) 1 9 3 4
=『Jazz Music Arrangement』(Japanese Translation by Shigeru Minami/Diichi Gakusya) 1 9 3 5

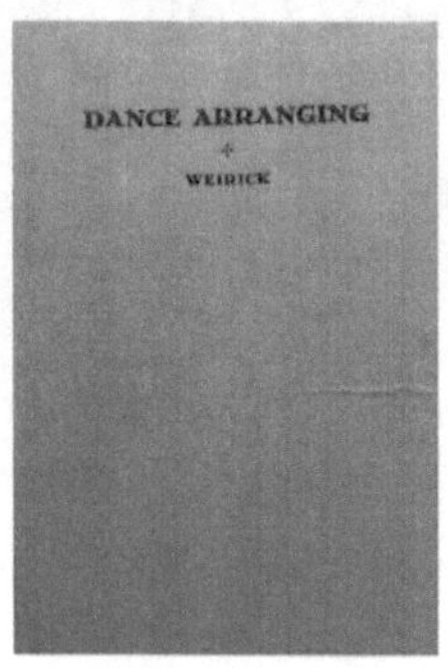

The original title is "Dance Arranging" and the Japanese translation in Japan is "Jazz Music Arrangement". Since the swing era jazz was also dance music, this title is satisfactory.

Anyway, it is a very good textbook. The book was published in 1934, but it doesn't look too old even now. After a brief introduction, the description of the instrument book, "Sax section", "Brass section", "Brass section" continues from the beginning. The "Rhythm section" from P18 shows the guitar chord work in detail. This is a feature that is not found in the text of the current arrangement method. The Harmony chapter from P45 begins with a detailed description of harmonization that describes how a triad smoothly resolves to the next chord, followed by an explanation of chords including 7th, diminished chords 9th and 11th, Harmonization by whole scale follows. From P72, writing by Duets and Torios is written about, for example, arranging when a piano is added to three saxophones.

The "Score" chapter from P81 is explained so that the role and balance of each instrument in the whole music can be understood.From P86, "Introduction" ("Wonder Bar", "Happiness Ahead", "Dames", "The Man on the Flying Trapeze", etc.) and "1st Chorus" ("The Very Thought" of You "How Can I be Blue"), "2nd Chorus", "VERSE" ("Congratulate Me"), "SPECIAL CHORUS") ("Carry me Back to Old Verginny", etc.), "LAST CHORUS" Is shown as an example of arrangement.

The chapter of "transposition" from P132 shows a method for performing smooth transposition based on the fourth degree circle indicating a close relation. After all, the textbooks more than 80 years ago are no longer the history of jazz, but a valuable legacy of music teaching materials.

In addition, as will be described in detail later, Yoshio Niki introduces this book in the book "Women's Pictorial Music Course 5: Light Music Techniques: First Volume" (Fujin Gaho Company).

『Ars Music Large CourseVol.9 TechniqueVersion : Jazz music – Playing method -Jazz piano 』(Shigeru Kikuchi、etc /ARS)1936

One of the authors, Shigeru Kikuchi, brought back a record of Dexieland Jazz from the United States in 1921 and is said to have played jazz for the first time in Japan in Kobe in the early Showa era.

This book seems to be his first jazz piano textbook written by Japanese. (For a Japanese translation book, " Vincent Lopez Modern Piano Method Book I" (「Vincent Lopez / Tokyo Ongakushoin」1936"))

In addition to the explanation of the chode, "Swing Base Table (in the above figure)", "Modern Harmony (the right in the above figure)", "Pentatonic" and "Blues" are also described.

Speaking of 1936, in the era when B-Bop (modern jazz) has not yet been born in the United States, this book is a textbook on how to play boogie-woogie and swing piano. Only the usage example of (13th) is written, but the content is very substantial as a whole. By the way, this book is written by Masao Koga, Ryoichi Hattori, Katsuhiko Haida, and others who have led the popular music in Japan. They were still in their late twenties and thirties. In that sense, it would be worth reading.

The titles of each author are as follows.
"History and current of jazz" (Ryutaro Hattori)
"Saxophone playing methods and practice songs" (Ryoichi Hattori)
"How to play jazz piano" (Shiji Kikuchi)
"Accordion Techniques and Practice Songs" (Masao Kogure)
"Guitar playing techniques and practice songs" (Masao Koga)
"How to play Hawaiian guitar and practice songs" (Harihiko Haida)
"Banjo playing techniques and practice songs" (Takashi Kakuda)
"Ukulele playing method and practice music" (Katsuhiko Haida)
"Key points of mandolin playing style" (Tanehiko Tanaka)
"Performance of various jazz percussion instruments" (Niki and others Yoshio)
"How to play minor harmonica" (Hideo Sato)
"Uta Hikata of popular songs" (Tokuyama II)
"Jazz Chorus" (Tadaharu Nakano)
"Types and Formats of Dance Songs" (Ichiro Ida)
"Organization and arrangement of jazz" (Kyosuke Paper)
"Talkies and Review Music" (Keizo Horiuchi)

『Method of Jazz piano』(Eiichi Yamada/Shinko Publication) 1947

A textbook published in 1947. That is the time when Be-Bop (modern jazz) has not yet entered Japan. Therefore, the textbook of boogie woogie and swing piano.

It's not much different from the Ars textbook introduced earlier, but is the new part such as the descending chromatic (including the 9th) chord and the practice of the Walking bass line (right in the above figure) with 8 jumps? Even so, this cover design is cool for this era.

『Fujin Gaho Music : Music Course Vol.5 : Popular Music Techniques Vol.1&.Vol.2』（Taizo Sugihara etc/（Fujin Gaho Company）1948〜49

Like the "Ars Music Large Course" introduced earlier, it is a very valuable textbook written by many people who have been leading Japanese popular music. There are two volumes, upper and lower, but with regard to jazz piano, Taizo Sugihara has written the title "Jazz Piano Playing Techniques" in the first volume on pages 131-153. When this book was published, it was when Be-Bop was finally born in the United States, so it probably would not have entered Japan yet. Therefore it is written about swing style piano playing.

A brief introduction to the content of Taizo Sugihara's writings, in Chapter 6, in Chapter 1 (P131-), states that the three synthetic elements in jazz are (theme), (musical instruments), and (players). And good jazz lies in crisp accents. "Emphasizes the importance of rhythm. Therefore, the second chapter (rhythmic rhythm: p132-) shows an example of performance using "walking bass" on the left hand, "triplet" on both hands, and "poly rhythm". Chapter 3 (melody melody: p140-) points out that the balance between dynamic sound and static sound (pause) is improvised and sophisticated. The fourth chord (Harmony: P143-) describes 36 codes of "Major, Major6th, Dominant7th, Minor, Minor6th, Minor7th, Diminith, Diminith7th". Also, the pattern riff for the left hand pattern riff of the boogie-woogie playing technique is shown, from A to Ab key, Ab to F key, and Cm to Bbm key. He also writes about "Implications for Voice-Leading", "Contra-motion", "Bad doubling", "Permissible doubling", Smooth "Jazz solution", and "Jazz Poly-Tonality". Chapter 5 (P150) points out the difference between classical and jazz "fingering". Chapter 6 (pages 151 to 153) shows an overall performance example over three pages.

The titles and author names other than Taizo Sugihara are as follows.

First volume: Jaz's arrangement (Kyosuke Kami), code (chords) (Itsuro Hattori), saxophone playing (Mitsuru Ashida), trumpet playing (Fumio Nanri), thrombon playing (Matsushi Taniguchi), string・Base playing method (Ryo Watanabe), playing method of jazz percussion instruments (Tanaka Tadao), reminiscence of jazz training (Ichiro Fujiyama), recollection of training (Shizuko Kasaki), memoir of jazz name player (Kabun Nogawa), Weiritz's arrangement method (Nikita Yoshio).
Second volume: Tango organization and arrangement (Munechi Yasushi), Hawaiian ensemble technique (Haruhiko Haida), accordion technique (Masao Kogure), Spanish guitar technique (Otosuke Ito), steel guitar technique (Bucky Shirakata) , Playing jazz guitar (Takashi Kakuda), playing ukulele (Haruhiko Haida), playing violin lightly (Kiyoshi Sakurai), playing harmonica (Nobuyoshi Nambu), singing tango (Tadao Takahashi), singing jazz (Betty Inada) Blues singing style (Noriko Awatani), jazz choir (Tadaharu Nakano) light music form (Kabun Nogawa), jazz history commentary [masterpiece commentary] (Ryutaro Hattori).

『How to Play Jazz Piano』(Hachiro/Zenon) 1953

This book was published when modern jazz began playing in Japan. But the content doesn't seem to be affected about it. A collection of songs with little theoretical explanation centered on Boogie and Swing Piano. The songs featured are as follows: 1. In terms of rhythm and tempo, "Vorn is a boat song", "Hungarian dance", "La Spanulas", "Spring song", etc. , "Arirang", "Bungawan Solo", "Anihirimele", etc. 3. "Firefly Light", "Rasasayan" etc. in the code 4. "Gypsy Moon", "Aroma" in the ad lib 5. "Jingle Bell" in the syncopation , "Valley Light", 6. "Passing Tone" "Caribbean Island", "Black Eyes", 7. "Blue Vest", "Coal Mine", and 8. Application Problems "Irish Daughter" Such. Jazz standard songs are not listed. Was there a copyright issue?

『Professional Arranger Composer: 1. 2 』(Russell Garci / Criterion Music Corp) 1954,1978

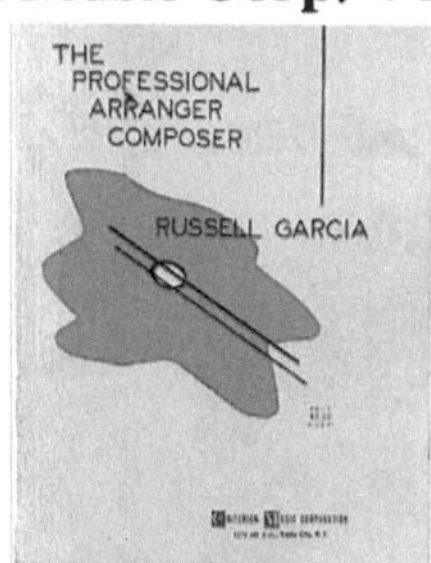

The left is the first volume published in 1954. One of the oldest and most famous books in jazz arrangements. In Japan, there were many composers and arrangers who used this book before Sadao Watanabe's jazz study was published. There are chapters from Book 1 to 6, but Book 1 starts with an explanation of the musical instrument's range, and is about pitches, chords, and basic harmony. Book2 is an ensemble of saxophone and rhythm instruments. Book3 is a small combo arrangement example. Book4 touches on the intro, composition between instruments, and ending, Book5 touches on alternative chords, surrogate chords, and melody writing, and Book6 touches on various variations on the original melody. Although it may be old, it is an excellent textbook that has already touched most of the important parts of the jazz arrangement in this era.

The right is a sequel to the same title, but it is not limited to jazz, but also describes the relationship between "Serie", "Free Improvisation", and "Art and Music". I think there are few people who are interested in art other than music. What is shown here is as simple as expressing the pitch and length by drawing. But the analogy of sound and painting is interesting and I think there may be more books like this. This book is also recommended for those interested in interactive art and media. By the way, the 1982 edition has a record, and the 2004 edition has a CD.

『Jazz Piano Chord Forms Book』(Hachidai Nakamura, Eiji Sawada /Shinko Music Publication) 1959

The left is the 1959 edition and the right is the 1960 edition. It is a jazz codebook, but it seems that such books were not published in Japan before this. A complex chord including tension (9th, 11th, 13th) has also been written, showing where on the keyboard it is drawn, with a graphical illustration of the keyboard. However, since the code is just piled up, it is not practical because it does not show how effective voicing is done with both hands, but it seems to be valuable as a dictionary for learning the code at the time.

『Jazz Improvisation 1 :Tonal and Rhythmic Principles 』 (John Mehegan/AMSC) 1959
=『The same Title』(Japanese Tranlation by Yo Aoi / Delbo) 1969

The book "Jazz Improvisation" is a famous book.
Probably the first full-scale textbook that systematically explained jazz. There are 4 volumes in all. This volume 1 shows examples of arpeggios and ad-libs based on the progression of chords in standard songs after explanation of the pitch, scale and chords. In particular, it is easy to understand that chord progressions are classified into three categories: II-V, diatonic, and chromatic.
 As for the piano, other than the harmony of the melody and Voting of Batto Powell's left hand, it is not particularly detailed. But as the title suggests, it's a great book to learn the principles of Jazz improvisation.

『LYDIAN CHROMITIC CONCEPTS』(George Russell/Concept Pub)1959= 『The same Title』(Japanese Tranlation by   Akihito Fuse,Yoshitaka Kjimoto/ATN)2005

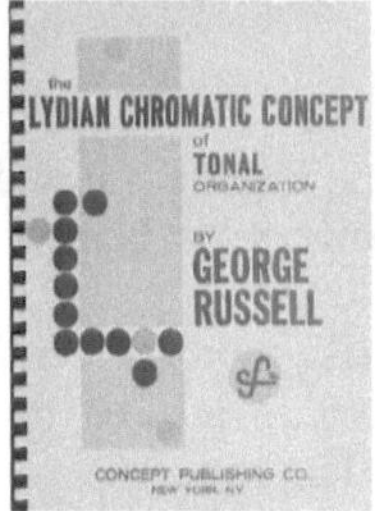 

A famous book, "LYDIAN CHROMITIC CONCEPTS" (hereinafter referred to as "LCC") has been said to have influenced Miles Divis mode playing and Toru Takemitsu's music. There seems to be a license to teach using this book. I haven't learned much in this book, so I may not be qualified to say much. For example, if a functional chode on a scale is considered to be vertical and a mode is considered to be horizontal, the functions of the sound system will be regularly distributed and the time will be ordered.

However, the LCC is neither vertical nor horizontal because the center of gravity is considered to be F instead of C in the case of a major scale. In other words, I think that "identity from differences" is a characteristic. Listen to the songs in Russell's "At Beethoven Hall" (SABA-Werke / 1965) made at LCC. At first, it is a repetition of the "difference" that can only be sensed with intensity to the "perceivable identical sound system", and gives stimulation. However, listening to a number of songs turns into something "sensible", that is, an object of recognition, and it gets a bit tired. If you are interested, please read this book. By the way, does the LCC still serve as a consensus for creating new music in the 21st century today?

『Adlib』(Higurashi Masanobu/Rhythm Echoes)1960

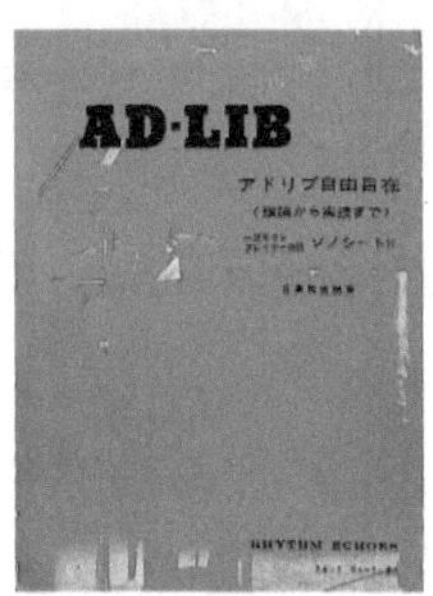  

The first edition was around 1960. Several revisions have been published. Since the publication year is not written, it is not known exactly.

However, the book on the left has a sonosheet (middle), so you can listen to the performance of Terumasa Hino when he was young. In any case, I think this book was published until about 80 years. Therefore, I think many people have learned in this book. Ad-lib is not wrong to play chords and scales as it is, but that's not good enough. Especially after the bebop (modern jazz), it is important for the performance to use the approach note based on the scale and chord. In this sense, this book shows a concrete example of how to make an ad-lib.

『COMPOSITION FOR THE JAZZ ORCHESTRA』(William Russo /University Of Chicago Press)1961

This is a book of only 90 pages, but the minimum techniques necessary to compose and arrange a big band with a focus on harmony are compactly compiled.

Speaking of compactness, is it like Gordon Jacob's orchestra in classical music? Perhaps such a book may be the only textbook needed to actually compose and arrange.

The important thing is that after studying with these textbooks, you will have as much contact with the actual score as possible.

『New Complete Edition Styles for the Jazz Pianist』John Mehegan /Sam Fox Publishing)1962

Mehegan's "modern piano style" is a textbook centered on the left hand Voicing, but this book is a textbook like an etude of a jazz piano. There are many practice songs by technique such as "Diatonic Pattern", "Chromatic Pattern", "Circle of Fifths Patterns". Among them, you will find block chord practice such as "The Minor Chord blocks", "The Half Diminished Chord Blocks", "The Diminished Chord Blocks". Since it is an etude textbook to the last, it is not interesting, but it may have been a good textbook for this era.

『Method For Jazz & Popular Arrengement』(Tsuruo Kageyama / Rhythm Echoes) 1963

Techniques necessary for arrangement such as chords, chord progressions, instrument methods, rhythm patterns, and harmony of session instruments have been shown some extend. However, it would probably be difficult to say that this book can be used to arrange popular music.

After all, the score of the arrangement example is only "Sakura, Sakura". Even considering the time when it was published in 1963, it would not seem to be of practical value unless a few examples of arrangements such as popular songs were shown

『PIANO JAZZ ALUBUM : Theme & Adlib』(Eiichi Ro/Kimeisya) Early 1960s(Presumption)

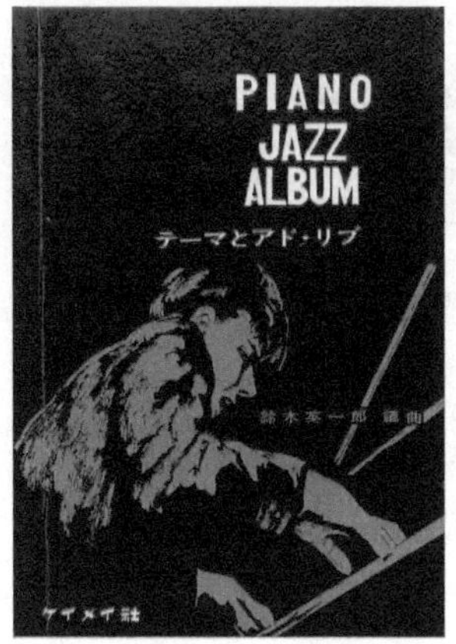

Since it is divided into three parts: Piano 1 "Melody" Part, Piano 2 "Ad-lib" Part, Rhythm (Piano, Guitar, Bass, etc) Part, this is a collection of songs that are supposed to be played in a trio.

The songs included "Side by Side", "The Saints Come to the City", "Indiana", "Humoresque", "Black Eyes", "Kushimoto Bushi", "Moon of Araki", and the original songs by the author.

Piano 1 is written in the original melody, and Piano 2 is written in jazz piano style. The left hand voicing isn't very jazzy, but the ad lib from the right hand can be used. In addition, only the chord name is written in Rhythm Part.

『Jazz pianoMethod : Basic Edition』(Hiroshi Iwasaki/ Kokusaigak ufu publishing) Early 1960s(Presumption)

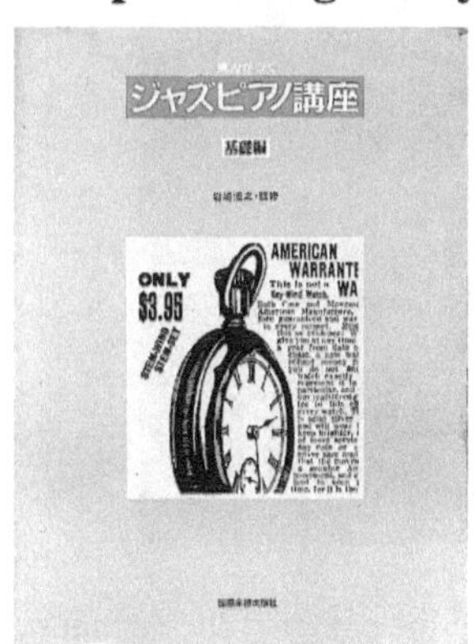

Up to P76, explanation of swing piano that allows the left hand to jump alternately. From P77 to P89, right-handed adlib practice.

A few ad lib examples from John Lewis, Sony Clark and Bud Powell are shown.

As an example of music, "Suzukake no kiri" and "Saint's march" are shown, and the walking baseline of the left hand may be helpful, but voicing used in modern jazz is hardly shown.

This book is a basic version, and seems to have a technical version, but it may be better.

『Contemporary Styles for the Jazz Pianist』 (John Mehegan /Sam Fox Publisher)1964

In short, it is a textbook that combines "New Complete Edition Styles for the Jazz Pianist" introduced earlier and "Jazz Improvisation 4" introduced later.
PART1 is a practice of various chords in the voicing style of Aform and Bform, which is explained in "Jazz improvisation 4".
PART2 practice PART1 chord work with various chord progressions.
PART3 is a practice song with styles such as RED GARLAND, WYNTON KELLY, HERBIE HANCOCK, MCCOY TYNER, BILL EVANS, KEITH JARRETT, PAUL BLEY, CECIL TAYLOR. It's better to use it together with "Jazz Improvisation 4".

『Swing and Early Progressive Piano Styles : Jazz Improvisation III』 (John Mehegan) 1965
＝『Jazz Professional Series Vol.1:Road to piano adlib』 (Ryo Hiraoka / Ongaku svunivu) 1971
＝『The same title 』 (Japanese Translation By Yo Aoi / Delbo) 1976

These three books are the same. The left is the original and the center is the Japanese translation, but it is not mentioned. The author is "Akira Hiraoka", so it may not be helped even if it is said to be plagiarism. On the right is an official (?) Japanese translation from Delvo. The contents are written about the swing-style piano style (Teddy Wilson, Art Tatum) and the style of early modern jazz (Bud Powell, George Shearing, Horace Silve). Teddy Wilson, Art Tatum, etc. have almost 10th left hand, so it's hard for Japanese to play. As a whole, there are mostly explanations on the left hand, and there are few descriptions about ad lib. But the George Shearing block code is very helpful.

Jazz Improvisation4:Contemporary Piano Styles』(John Mehegan/AMSC)1965 =『The Same Title』(Japanese Translation By Yo Aoi / Delbo) 1976

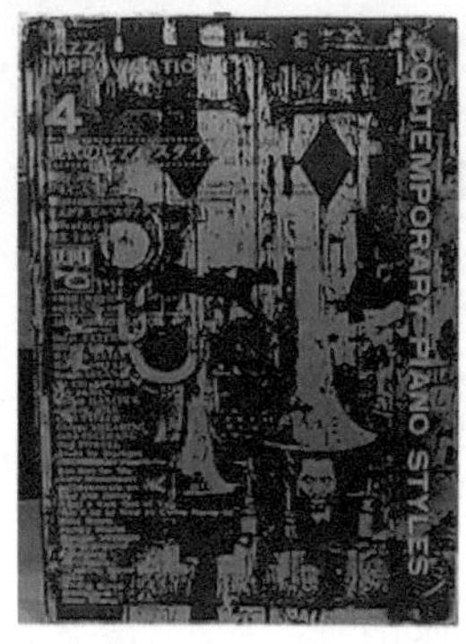

No book in jazz piano has influenced as many jazz pianists as this book. I wanted to play a jazz piano, and I had used several books until then, but none of them was satisfactory, but when I encountered this book and played it, the "jazz sound" was heard from the first page and finally " "I can play jazz piano," I remember.

The book is quite thick, but the code work is divided into A form and B form depending on the type. However, since this textbook itself is centered on the left-hand voice voicing, it is not possible to grasp all the chord work of jazz piano with this book alone. There are also block codes, compings, and explanations of the left-hand arpeggio, but Adlib has Bill Evans Transcription on the whole, but there are few.

『Jazz Impressions Of New York(Dave Brubeck / TOA Music Publisher)1 9 6 6

Bluebeck is an intelligent jazz man who studied composition with Schoenberg and Myo. At that time, it was very popular with Ivy League students. Speaking of Bluebeck, it is a series of impressions such as "Journey" jazz represented by "Take Five" and "Europe", "Japan", "USA". This song collection "Impression of New York" is one of those impression series, written for the TV drama "Mr. Broadway".

There is no ad-lib posting, only themes, but voicing of block codes is very useful. By the way, as an appendix, "Toki's Theme Toki no Theme" from "Impression of Japan" is included in the first song (4P) for some reason (not in the table of contents of this book). And "Upstage Rumba" is a unique song written in 12-tone technique based on Latin rhythm. It may be an influence learned by Schoenberg.)

『 Jazz Piano Technique VoL.1 Popular Piano Edition 』
（Masanobu Higurashi／Rhythm Echoes）late1960ₛ (Presumption)

This "Jazz Piano Technique" has two volumes, a popular piano edition and a modern jazz edition. This is the former. In general, the term popular piano has been around for a long time. They have the image of playing pops, easy listening, and screen music on the piano. Music like "Paul Mauriat", "Richard Clayderman", "Andre Gagnon" would be exactly the name popular piano. However, since such music can be easily played once you have mastered a jazz piano, you can think of the popular piano as a pre-stage of jazz piano. The content of this book is very different from the image of such a popular piano. Based on boogie woogie and swing-style piano performance before modern jazz. R & B and rock piano styles are also shown. That said, it is too simple and has little practical value. It also describes Latin-style playing techniques, which is probably because Japanese pop songs have been influenced by Latin music for some time. However, it is too simple, and it is different from the "Latin Jazz Piano" playing technique that we say today.

『Jazz Piano Technique VoL.2 Modern Jazz Edition』
（Masanobu Higurashi ／Rhythm Echoes） late1960(Presumption)

This is a modern jazz version of "Jazz Piano Technique". This is probably the first textbook written about techniques after Be-Bop in Japan. Since Chord work is not explained from the beginning, it seems to be a textbook for intermediate students. There are various examples of chord progressions and Substitute chords, but all of them were too abrupt and difficult to understand. Although many jazz textbooks were published from Rhythm Echoes, I think there were few practical ones from the 1960s to the 1970s. (It still seems to be sometimes exhibited at Yahoo! Auctions etc.)

『PIANO CHORD&AD-LIB ENCYCLOPEDIA』
(Toshiharu Honda／Tokyo Gakufu Publisher）late1960(Presumption)

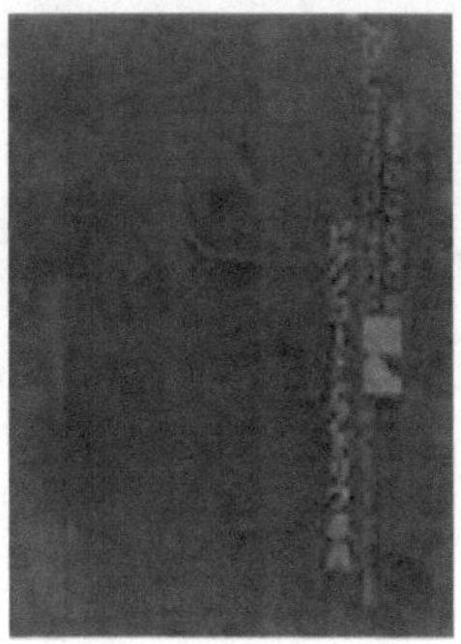

An ad-lib example is shown based on the chord. Music is also a kind of language, although it is more abstract than everyday language. What is important is the connection between words, that is, chord and chord.

Therefore, even if you master ad lib with one chord, it will be difficult to find meaning and value there.

In ad lib, the relationship between chord and chord, phrases and phrases, that is, relationships is important.

『JazzChord : Theory & Instruction』(Higurashi Masanobu/ Rhythm Echoes）late1960(Presumption)

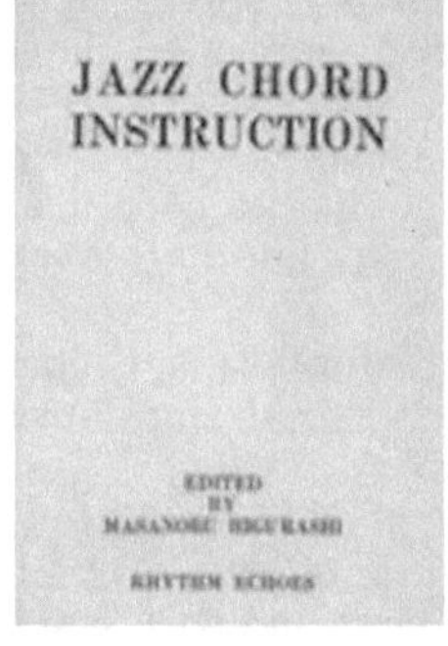

Starting from the pitch, it is a learning book of basic music theory such as scale, chord, chord progression, cadence, substitute chords, various chord progressions, cyclic chords, how to interpret chords for melodies. However, there is almost no description of the voicing and harmonization actually used in jazz. This is a typical example of the jazz textbooks that were published in Japan during the time this book was published.

『Jazz Chord Understand quickly : How to play jazz piano』(Masanobu Higurashi／Rhythm Echoes）1960s

In short, it is a textbook of Rag Time and Boogie Woogie.

From the first part to the third part. The first part is about the code. It is explained by comparing the keyboard diagram with the staff. However, how to do effective codework with both hands is very basic. The second part is a left-handed jump, or practice of lag time. The third part is Rag Time and Boogie's practice song.

In the commentary of this book, it is written that "If you use this book, the basics of ad lib are completed."Really?

『Modern Adlib Passage Chord Progression』(Higurashi Masanobu) late1960(Presumption)

This book shows examples of adlib based on various keys.
There are also some adlib such as Oscar Peterson, Sony Clark, Charlie Parker, Horace Silver, Sony Rollins, Wes Montgomery and Stan Getz.
The chord progression table for each key is posted at the end of the book.
Such a book is now commonplace, but at the same time it would have been practical.

『Modern Jazz:Theory & Practice』(Masanobu Higurashi / Rhythm Echoes) late1960(Presumption)

It is written about chords including tension and substitute chords from the beginning, and the following P6 to P9 show melodies and ad lib examples by chromatic chord progression, but they are abrupt.
P12 contains 8 bars of comping examples. P13 to 17 are written as general dominant motion, composite code, and blues chord . P18 is written as ad-lib solo, but there is no score, Just an explanation.
P19 has a whole scale. P21-23 has a code for the pianist, but there is no description of the code name, to the extent shown as a reference example,
Examples of modern jazz songs include "Theme of the Sun Season", "Moon and Boy", and "Zero Collection".P31 to 39 are written about various rhythms of jazz。 Overall, the contents of this book are halfway. Among them, the basic code and code index from P40 may have some practical value.

『Jazz Piano Standrd Method』(TsuRuo Kageyama / Rhythm Echoes) late1960(Presumption)

It starts with an explanation of triads, and is written about 7th chords, dominant chords, diminished chords, 11th chords, and 13th chords. However, it is not written how to make effective chord work with both hands just by building up sounds.
From P11 to P41, it describes how to play a swing piano and boogie that the left hand jumps. P42 and 43 are mambo-style playing techniques, P46 and 47 are blues playing techniques with boogie woogi, and only 3 pages from P48 to 51 are written about modern jazz piano playing, but the left hand is only a single note.

『 H o w T o P l a y J a z z P i a n o 』 (Motohiro Suzuki/Nichion) 1967

Chapter 1 is written about pitch, scale, chord, and chord progression in general.

Chapter 2 includes ad-lib techniques including approach notes, jazz form, and basic rhythms such as swing bass, Western rhythm, Rock & Roll Rhythm, syncopated rhythm, walking bass, folk rhythm, rolling bass boogie, rumba. I feel nostalgic because it also contains rhythms that are no longer used, such as Begin.

From P58, it is written about 4th chords used in modern jazz, poly chords, chords including 9th, 11th, 13th, semitone progression, full tone progression. You can feel history such as saying polycode as "multi-chords" and semitone progression as "semitone step progression". In the jazz textbook of the publisher of this book, it will fall into the category of good books.

『Jazz Play Basic Knowlegs』(Tsuruo Kageyama / Rhythm Echoes) late1960(Presumption)

Chapter 1 is written about pitch, scale, chord, and chord progression in general.

Chapter 2 includes ad-lib techniques including approach notes, jazz form, and basic rhythms such as swing bass, Western rhythm, Rock & Roll Rhythm, syncopated rhythm, walking bass, folk rhythm, rolling bass buki, rumba. It also contains rhythms that are no longer heard, such as Begin.

From P58, it is written about 4th chords used in modern jazz, poly chords, chords including 9th, 11th, 13th, Chromatic progression, and whole tone progression. Although we feel the times, such as "poly chord" as "poly chord" and "Chromatic step progression" as semitone progression, it will fall into the category of good books among the jazz textbooks that published this book.

『Jazz Piano Method : Basic Edition』(Tokyo Jazz Society /Kokusai Gakufu Publisher)late1960(Presumption)

At the beginning, the figure of the keyboard shows where the chord is played. Next, the diatonic codes used for each key from P11 to 16 are posted. Next, rhythm patterns such as waltz, tango, bolero, biggin, rumba are posted on pages 17-20. After that, the ragtime playing method in which the left hand plays the Root and triads alternately and the 5th and triads continues until the second half. Although there is a little description about the phrase how to ad lib, it is about touch. There are only a few phrases from John Lewis, Bud Powell and Sony Clark on the right hand . I cannot deny the feeling of a halfway book.

『Modern Jazz Harmony』(Seiji Kitano/ Rhythm Echoes) late1960(Presumption)

This book is a incomplete textbook.
Since it starts with the pitch, if you think it is a textbook for first-time learners, you will suddenly go to the next page, where you can see examples of harmony and arrangement of Stan Kenton and Count Basie, Greek and Medieval Church. There are explanations of modes such as diminish scale, full scale, pentatonic, etc., but the examples of music using them are fragmentary. Still, on the page called Atonity and John Coltrane and Ornette Coleman, Coleman's "Chapaca Suite" shows a few bars and I have a good feeling that the author says, "I recommend listening to some songs called New Jazz played by Don Cherry." But at the same time I couldn't help laughing.about it. In any case, this is a textbook that the author had a hard time writing.

『Jazz Composition and Orchestration』 (William Russo/University of Chicago Press) 1968

Author William Russo is a composer and trombone player. His work was also performed in the Stankenton Orchestra. It is also known for the field of third-stream music that combines classical and jazz. His concerto, based on the sound of a harmonica as a cry of a cat, is played by the San Francisco Symphony Orchestra conducted by Seiji Ozawa and made into an album.He has worked on many unique and diverse works. This book is 843 pages (although difficult to read in handwriting), but rather than a textbook on jazz composition / arrangement, it is an expression / music theory to learn about the activities of such various Russo music.It is interesting to note that this book has 82 pages of cello, but apparently he has a jazz orchestra work that includes four cellists.

『MODERN JAZZ SCHOOL』 (Yo Aoi / Delbo) 1968、1969

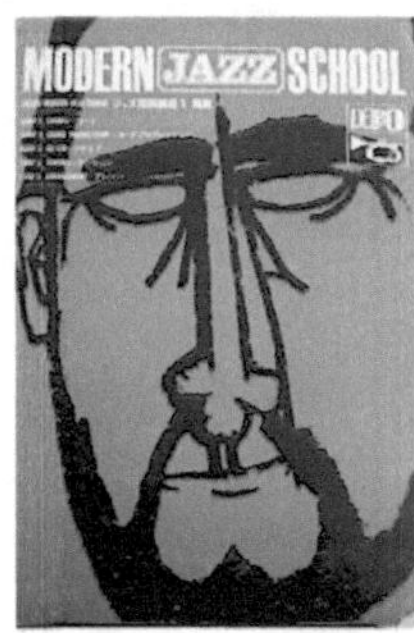 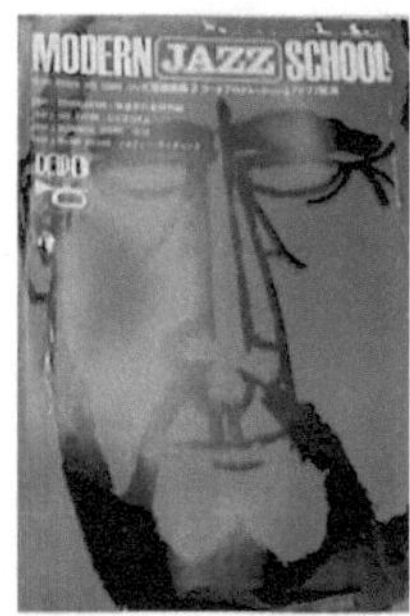

The main contents of Volume 1 are "chord" and "chord type", "chord progression", "substitute chord", "advanced approach note and approach note harmony", "tension", and "arrangement" Just then. The harmony of "tension" is not very detailed. Count Basie's score is posted as an example score. Since this book was published in the late 60s, authors should also post newer orchestra scores.

Volume 2 is first written about pitch, cadence, diatonic chords, substitute chords, and forms. Next, about 20 pages of jazz rhythm are written, but this is detailed.

And from P61, it is written that you should practice chord study and tension, but it is just a stack of chords and no practical chord work.

The overall jazz form is detailed, but there is no clear explanation for the practical harmony and examples of the relationship between code and adlib.

At the end of the book are examples of ad libs by Herbie Man, Attila Zoller, Lee Morgen and Miles Davis.

『Jazz Study』(Sadao Watanabe/Nichion）1970

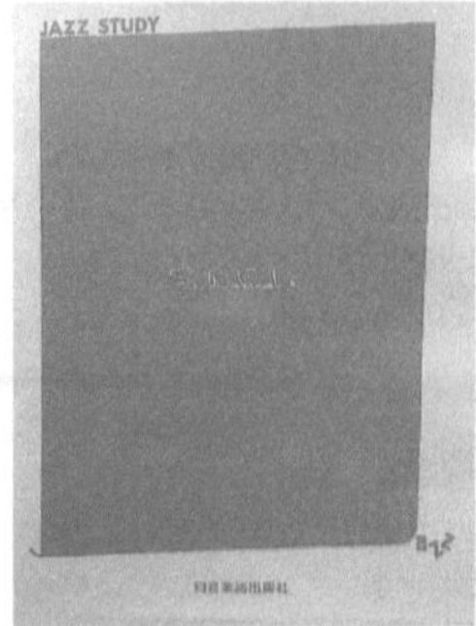

This is a very famous textbook in Japan, so I may not need to mention it anymore. Anyway, many musicians learned from this book.

By the way, I bought this book when I was in my second year of high school. As expected, it was incomprehensible to me as a high school student. However, I was surprised to hear that the actor "Enari kazuki" was studying in this book when he was a junior high school student.

The content is an Arrangement textbook with a focus on harmonization. It is not a book about ad lib. It will not be understood without knowledge of code and scale at a minimum. Learning this book from beginning to end will help you. But you need patience.

『JAZZ PIANO METHOD VOL.1,2』(Eiichi Fujii/Rhythm Echoes) Around1970(Presumption)

Eiichi Fujii has published a considerable number of jazz piano textbooks to date, and I think this book is a book when it falls into the early category. It may have been published until around 1980. By the way, I feel like the first jazz piano textbook I bought was this book.

There must be many people learning from this book, but how effective was this book to study jazz piano? To put it simply, I think it was an effective book for learning to get used to jazz piano.

Although it is divided into blues and standard (only the adlib part is not included), the blues is designed to play using only one blues scale, which is effective for jazz piano beginners I think that's the way. For the standard, only a single note (main tone) is posted on the left hand. On the right Hand is a lot of typical Be Bop phrase.

Therefore, even if you do not understand the theory, you can experience the feeling of jazz even if you play it roughly.

『6 Books in 1 Encyclopedia of Improvisation』
(Walter Stuart、Bugs Bower、Stan Applebaum /Charles Colin)1970

This book is a collection of 6 books originally. Although there are few theoretical explanations, as a whole, it is detailed about Approach note and Passing tone for ad lib.

It also touches on scales that are not used much in jazz, such as "12 tone technique", "How to Constract And Use New Artifucal Scales", "Modern New Scales". It's not particularly a textbook, but it might be good to know how to make an ad lib.

『Piano modern adlib technique』(Hiroshi Iwasaki/Ongaku syunjyu)1970
『Jazz piano modern adlib』(Hiroshi Iwasaki/Ongaku syunjyu)1974

The title and cover of the two books are different, but the content is the same. Looking at the cover of the photos of Oscar Peterson and Ma Waldron, it seems like a full-fledged jazz piano textbook, but the actual content is nothing but symbolic

The songs included "Love is blue", "Jours en France", "Bube's love", " The House of the Rising Sun", " I Left My Heart in San Francisco"", and "Autumn leaves". There is no jazz ad lib in particular.

And there are also photos of Chick Korea and Freera Prim that are unrelated to the content of the book (bitter smile). In Japan Until the early 1970s, it can be said that this textbook is a typical example of a jazz piano.

『JAZZ ORGAN Theory&Practice：From Chord To Jimmy Smith』 (Isao Asanuma/Rhytum Echoes) Around1970

I think that the number of jazz organ textbooks is less than that of the piano, but if you include the most electon textbooks, it will be a huge number, but I think that the organ here is the textbook of Hammond Organ. The contents include basic chord and chord explanation, intro, ending, fill-in examples, phrases born from typical chord progressions, etc. The feature is jazz organ guru, Jimmy · It will be an analysis of Smith's performance. The contents are "Chapter 6 Jimmy Smith's Blues Chord", "Chapter 7 Jimmy Smith's Blues Sound", and "Chapter 8 Jimmy Smith's Sound Transcription".

The textbook that explains Jimmy Smith's performance in detail is a valuable textbook because it seems to be the first in Japan.

『FIRST CHART』 (Jimmie Haskell /Criterion Music Corp) 1971, with Records。

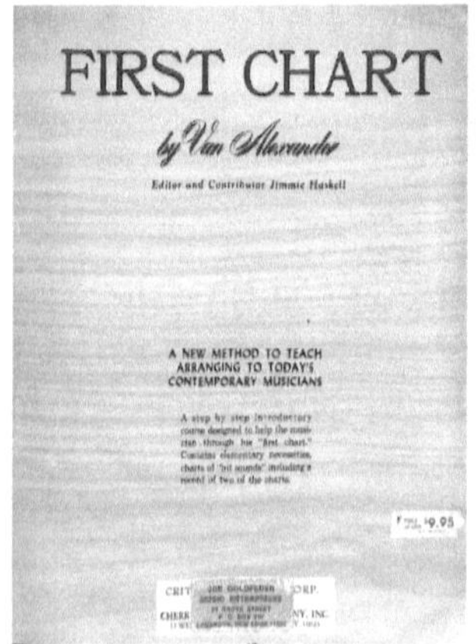

I think it's a little-known textbook in Japan, but it will be in the category of good books. The main contents consist of "instrument method", "VOICING","rhythm section", "music analysis", and "combination section".

Although it is not very detailed about harmonization, it explains the technique necessary for arranging the song "MOONLIGHT IN VERMONT" using 30 pages (P67 ~ 97). There are many textbooks that explain a lot of short samples, but the method like this book is good in that it understands the structure of the whole song.

『Jazz Theory World of Fouth Chords』(Seiji Kitano/Rhythm Echoes) Early1970s(Presumption)

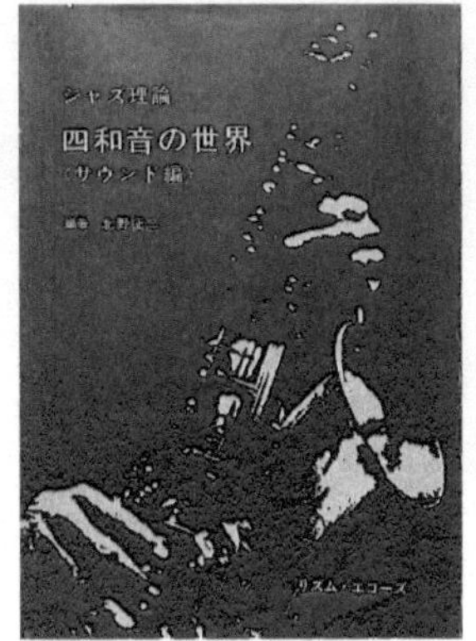

In other words, the title of "The world of four chords" can be said to be "Jazz harmony method with four voices".

Starting with the pitch, it covers all the theories necessary for jazz such as chord progression, surrogate chords, tensions, approach notes, poly chords, organ points, and blue notes.

But all are halfway. It's written for first learners because it explains from the pitch, but it's not easy to understand. For example, although "tension" is described in P60 to P63, only two codes are written as an example. There are also descriptions that confuse the use of scale and mode.

『Jazz Rock Orchestra Sound & Scores』(Masaichi Hirose／Taiyo Music Company)1972, with Records

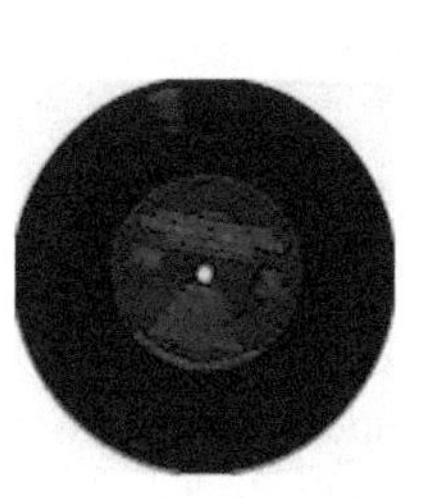

Includes 3 records. It must have been groundbreaking at the time of release. Harmonize is written in detail for each section such as trumpet, trombone, saxophone. Looking at this textbook, it reminds me of the old days when the jazz big band played the back of the singer.

『Atene Popular Music Series Education Course～Let's play Popular Piano～Beginner, Intermediate,Advanced』 （Hiroshi Kuroki, Kazuo Yashiro/ Atene Music）1972

This book is correspondence text book for learning popular piano.
"Songbook", "Theory text" and "6 records" are included in the set.
It was an epoch-making teaching material at that time, where you could learn popular piano while listening to records.
The above is an intermediate version. Since there was only an intermediate version at the time of release, there is no particular description of the grade.
Later, "Beginner", "Intermediate" and "Advanced" courses were created.
By the way, every time the grade goes up, it becomes jazzy, but the advanced edition is supervised by jazz pianist Kazuo Yashiro. The school course also had an "Athens Popular Piano School" at Ginza in Tokyo.

『SOUNDS and SCORES』（HENRY MANCINI/Cherry Lane Music）1973

Henry Mancini's orchestration book using his own songs. It is a very good textbook for those who aim to compose and arrange music. At the time I purchased it, a Japanese translation of this book had not yet been released. This book had three records, but now comes with a CD. By the way, many musicians recommended this book more than Sadao Watanabe's "Jazz Study". The content highlights the characteristics of the various instruments and explains how they are arranged in actual music. "MR.Lucky Theme", "Peter Gun", "Softly" when using French Horn. "Blues For Mother's" or "Joanna" when using a brass session of Trumpet and Trombones, "Night Flower" for Marimba. "Lightly latin" when using Basson. When using Flute and Piccolo, "Timothy" and so on. Through this book, learners will be able to learn a lot of things necessary for arrangement.

『The Contemporary Arranger』(Don Sebesky/Alfred Music)1974

This book is a masterpiece of the Arrangement Method textbook. Don Seveski is famous as a composer / arranger who made CTI sound with Creed Taylor. Sevesky points out the four elements necessary for the arrangement: It is "Balance" (Tone balance, form balanceetc), Economy (Is the art of omitting anything from the score not absolutely necessary), "Focus" (Points within an arrangement where individual element is more important than any other), Variety (Formal list of instrumental combination). 288 examples with different instrumentation are shown. Previously, this book was an appendix to the record, but the current edition comes with a CD, which will give you great hints on how to create the effective sound needed for your arrangement.

『Jazz Piano method』(Kaoru Iiyoshi / Zenon)1974

This book contains a lot of chord works and ad lib, so it's good to hone the basics of jazz piano. Still, most of the chord works is listed only up to 7th.

The chord works actually used in jazz performances is about six bars on page 36. Why didn't you post more? That said, Adlib was pretty helpful because it included a phrase that seems to be Bud Powell's Transcription (although this book is rarely seen recently).

『JAZZ /ROCK VOISINGS for the CONTEMPORARY KEYBOARD PLAYER 』(Don Haerle/STUDIO P/R) 1974

Although it is only a 40-page textbook, it is a good book that is comparable to John Megan's "modern piano style" 288-page book.

Compared to John Megan's classification of Voicing into A form and B form, this book classifies Voicing into A form, B form and C form. In addition, John Megan's textbook has little description of chord works with both hands, and there is little mention of modal voicing, but this book details them. It is a very valuable textbook.

『 Practical Popular Music Arrangment 』 (Genichi Kawakami /Yamaha Music Shinkoukai)1974

A large dictionary of arrangements unparalleled in the world. I think there was a separate workbook with a record, but I didn't buy it. The book's advertising ad certainly says "For those who must arrange by tomorrow".

In other words, this book shows that any arrangement is possible.

Anyway, this is a detailed book. The issue is in 1974. I don't hear about the revised version. I still think that this book has practical value, but at least it's still valid for music, harmony and orchestration. However, there are some parts that are really old. For example, this book states that "synthesizers are monophonic instruments". In fact, it is a textbook from the analog era. In the past, it was possible to arrange most popular music by learning jazz theory. There were also many pop composers from jazz pianists such as Kyohei Tsutsumi.

However, now it will be difficult to express cutting-edge music with just jazz theory. Since the computer became indispensable for music production, the rhythm and timbre have changed particularly. Especially for timbres, it is impossible to represent various electronic sounds made on a PC with staff paper. In short, in addition to popular music theory like this book, IT knowledge such as PC, electronic sound, and programming is indispensable.

『Play Bach: Jacques Loussier』 (Jacques Loussier / Carisch Products) 1974

Speaking of playing classical classics in jazz, the names Jack Jacques and Eugen Cicero soon come to mind. In terms of jazziness, I think it's Cicero, but when it comes to artistry, Ruchet may be better. In the case of Luce, most of the time he specialized in jazzing Bach (although he also plays Debssy and Sati), why do we play Bach in a jazz style? Generally, when performing classical classical music in jazz, it is common to play the theme and then play the adlib jazzy. However, polyphonic music such as baroque music has no master-slave relationship in each voice, and baroque music was often improvised. So when we played Bach in jazz, we might have thought that we could naturally transition to jazz without breaking the original song. Published songs include Prelude, Invention, Toccato and Fugue. There is also an appendix with bass scores.

『JAZZ PIANO IMPROVOSATION Vol.1～3』 (Sadayasu Fujii /Rittor Music) 1975

A transcription textbook of the performances of people such as McCoy Tyner, Chick Corea and Winton Kelly. There are 3 volumes in all. After publishing these textbooks, he published practical jazz textbooks one after another, such as "Jazz Piano Mode Playing Method" (Ritto Music) and "Improvisation Techniques Practiced with the Keys of Jazz Piano 12" (Ritto Music). Issued. Just as the Berlin Wall collapsed, it can be said that the collapse of the jazz textbook in Japan was done by Sadayasu Fujii.

So why wasn't a practical jazz piano textbook published in Japan until then? I think there are several reasons for this. For one thing, because the essence of jazz is improvisation, it seems that there was a sense of resistance to using sound as a score like classical music. Furthermore, with classical music, even if the music system and overall picture are shown by the score, considerable training is required to play difficult songs. However, in the case of jazz, as long as you know the playing methodology, you can play even if you don't have any technique. Therefore, anyone who knows how to play jazz can play jazz (although it is not). Then it will be a problem as a professional musician. Therefore, he may have wanted to keep the performance method as secret as possible.

『JAZZ IDIOM』（Jerry Coker/Prentice Hall）1975
＝『JAZZ IDIOM : Basics Of Performance And expression』（Japanese
Translation ByTakefusa Sasamori/Ongakuno Tomosya）1978

In short, it is a book written about learning jazz. (However, there is some practical work on keyboard chode work. (It also describes the modal voicing used in "So What") The author offers advice on a variety of issues, but the key points are as follows.

"If the ad-lib phrase becomes monotonic, use chromatic scales. But before that, new patterns, substitute chords and scales, newer variants of chords and scale structures (some from foreign music culture), rhythm-metric-accent techniques, motif developments, new horizons to study Exciting progression, listening to even more performers. I'll renew my practice and interpretation when it's going to be monotonous. "

I think that's exactly the case, but if you want to add more, take a break (do not play), and, related to the chromatic scale, use blue notes.

『Pentatonic Scales for Jazz Improvisation 』（The Ramon　Ricker /Alfred Music）1975

Pentatonic, like the major and minor scales, does not have a clear master-slave relationship, so the performer can freely ad-lib, making it easier for first learners to perform. At the same time, because it tries to release from the complex harmony, it is also often used for advanced ad lib.

Examples include "Datonic Exercise", "Chromatic Exercise", "Exercise in Dominant Motion", "Exercise in Circle 5th", "Alternated Pentatonic Exercise", etc. Reference examples include Joe Farrell, Wayne Shorter, Joe・Examples of ad lib from Henderson, Chick Korea and Herbie Hancock are shown.

『THE SOUND OF IMPROVISATION』(MikeCarubia/Alfred Publishing) 1976

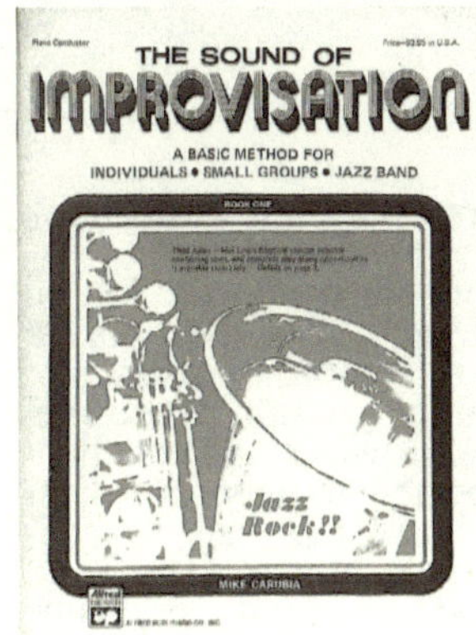

It is written as a basic method for individuals, small groups, and Jazz band, but it can also be used as a piano self-study.

There is a separate melody part along with the piano comping part. "Single note melody in Right Band", "Melody Played in Octaves with 5th", "Improvised Right hand in Single Notes", "Improvised Right Hand with Octaves And 5th" Since the style is posted, you can practice comping or ad lib practice. Because it is a simple song overall, it can be recommended for first-time learners.

『Practical Seminar Of Jazz-Vol.Theory Edition』(Sadayasu Fujii//Rittor Music) 1976
『The Same Title Vol.2 Arrange Edition』(You Kitagawa/Rittor Music) 1986

Volume 1 is a book for first learners to learn about chords, chord progressions, scale modes, etc. starting from the pitch. Since it is in a workbook format that includes exercises, jazz theory is acquired while writing.

For example, it can be said that it is a basic book of the theory necessary for composing and arranging like writing a substitute code for the diminished code for each key.

Volume 2 describes how to harmonize a few bands or more than 6 parts of a big band. Unlike Volume 1, it is not a workbook. I get the impression that it is like a musical composition analysis book. There is a lot to learn because it is a fairly detailed analysis. However, in today's era when PCs are indispensable for composition and arrangement, the importance of rhythm and tone is increasing. Therefore, arrangement can be done without learning harmony so much.

『The Erroll Garner Song Book』(Sy Johnson, ErrollGarner/ Cherry lane Music)1977

There are many types of Erroll Garner's song book, but I think this book is the most complete.
His famous song "Misty" is played on the key of Ab in his first album. Generally, it is often played with the key of Eb, but in this book, two songs of Eb and G are published. On the youtube video site, Garner played with C's key. However, an excellent musician like Garner will be able to play regardless of Key. Since it is a song book, there are few ad-lib descriptions, but you may be able to experience "behind the beat" unique to Garner and a gorgeous performance with lots of decorative sounds.

『Contemporary Jazz piano1・2』(Yasutoshi Inamori & Naohiko Hojo/ ChyouArt)1977、1980

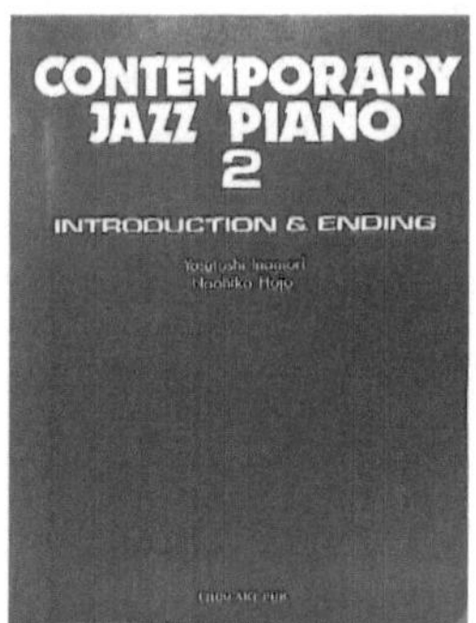

There is a first volume and a second volume. The first volume is divided into "Theory" and "Improvisation". In "Theory", as "Analyze of Ad-lib Phrase", "Diatonic Phrase", "Diminished Phrase", "Chromatic Phrase", "Blue Note Scale", "Phrase with Perfect Force", "Pentatonic Phrase" Phrases "and other examples of ad libs used in jazz are all shown, so it can be used as a reference for progressive performances such as playing freely. In the latter half of "Improvisation", the score is a complete Transcription of the performances of Oscar Peterson, Bill Evans and Winton Kelly, but the scale and chord work used are also analyzed in detail. Therefore, it will be very convenient for learners.

Volume 2 is titled as a textbook about intro and ending, but it explains in detail about chord progression, substitute chords, etc. I'm wondering why this is the second volume. Rather, considering the contents, I think this should have been the first volume. Also, as examples of intros and endings, various examples of pianists such as Hampton Hawes, Peter Nero, Andre Prepin, George Shearing, etc. are posted abundantly, so it will be helpful for rehamonisation. And as an example of "improvisation," performances by Bill Evans, Red Garland, and Herbie Hancock are posted.

『Let's Play Jazz PianoVol.1〜4』(Teru Sakamoto/Ongakunotomosya) 1977〜78

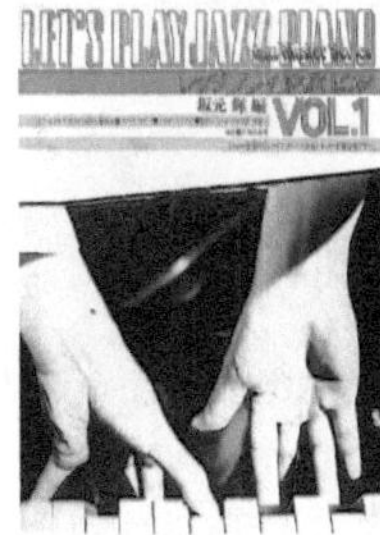  

Author Teru Sakamoto aka Terry Harman. While active as a jazz pianist, he has a long career as an educator. He has been teaching jazz piano since the age of 21.

"Teru Sakamoto Jazz Piano Workshop"in Jazz magazine was a very interesting seminar in a novel style, but this published textbook was a total of 4 volumes and became a hot topic in the jazz textbook (?). By the way, I went to a certain jazz school for about 3 months, but at that time it was this book that I used at school. I felt like I could improvise if I played the "Autum leaves" of Vol.1 every day. No difficult theory is written. It is a textbook that says to play anyway. A record to be used with this book was also released by Victor.

『Bud Powell: Jazz Masters Series』(Clifford J. Safane/ Music Sales Amer) 1978
『Thelonious Monk: Jazz Masters Series』(Stuart Isacoff/Music Sales Corp) 1978

Two pianists who can be said to be the founders of modern jazz piano.
Bud Powell's piano in particular is an exemplary material for those who play jazz piano.

Unfortunately, it is only the theme that shows the performance of both hands. The ad lib part is only the right hand.

The songs include "Hallucinations", "A Night in Tunisia", "Strictly Confidential", etc.

Thelonious Monk is a unique pianist. Intriguing phrases, chords, and ironic expressions. For that reason, some fans are enthusiastic about him and others say that they are not good at it. Also, if you think that Teddy Wilson's piano is reminiscent, you might feel free jazz pianos such as Cecil Taylor. The songs are "Off Minor", "I Mean You", "Rudy My Dear", "In Walked Bud", etc

『Jazz Improvisation for Keyboard Players:Complete』(Dan Haerle/Columbia Pictures Pubns）1978

You can learn ad lib that has been upgraded gradually, starting from simple ad lib with code and scale. There are no modal ad-libs or out-phrases, but they are very easy to understand and can be recommended for beginners.

Most of them are written in C key, so if you play in various keys, you will improve your skills considerably.

『Jazz & Popula:Theory& Practice』(Junichi Kaneko/Art Music）1978

Author Keiichi Kaneko is from the Tokyo University of the Arts and a professor at Shobi Gakuen University. There is a unique study that considers the thoughts of Jack Derrida and Deleuze through his own work "The last leaf" in his thesis (Bulletin of "Musical Ideas", Shobi Gakuen Junior College).

Although this book is a thin book of about 70 pages, you can learn about "Chord Progression", "Substitute Chord", and "Harmonization" starting from the pitch. It is like a workbook, there are many excises, and there are examples of answers, so it is good for first learners.

『The Contemporary Jazz Pianist』（Bill Dobbins /GAMT Music Press）1978

This book has up to 4 volumes. Briefly introduce each volume.

The first volume is left hand voicing, and the code that is often used in jazz is written from the beginning like the book of John Megan. This is followed by surrogate chords and rehearsalization, right hand phrase exercises, Diatonic, Pentatonic, Diminish, and Chromatic.

Volume 2 is Voicing with both hands, ad-lib exercises in the blues, then "Rhythm Changes", "Popular song form", "Ballard Style", "Jazz Rock Style", "Latin Style", "Contemporary Form", "Free Jazz", "Comping", etc.

Volume 3 includes "Stride Piano Style", "Boogie Woogie Piano", 'Gospel Piano', "Bi Bupp Piano Style", "Solo Ballad Style", "1960s, 70s Harmonic Style", "Latin and Ostinato" Various styles such as "Style" and "Free Jazz" are written.

Volume 4 is "Scott Joplin", "Jelly Roll Morton", "Earl Hines Teddy Wilson", "Duke Ellington", "Art Tatum", "Thelonious Monk", "Bud Powell", "Oscar Peterson", "Erroll Garner" Author of famous jazz pianist styles such as "Lennie Tristano", "Bill Evans", "Clare Fischer", "Jimmy Rowles" "Cecil Taylor", "Chick Corea", "Keith Jarrett", "Richie Beirach" Of Dobbins has posted a song imitated.

One of the features that other textbooks don't have is that they mention free jazz piano style in Volumes 2, 3 and 4. In particular, Volume 3 categorizes free jazz into "Bent", "Vortex", "Shadows", and "Mobile" based on Paul Bray's style, and shows it in his own songs by Dobbins. , Dobbins is a discordant cluster block code referring to Cecil Taylor's "Fly! Fly! Fly!", "Garden", and "Silent Tongues", and a technique using a chord with a chromatic parallel progression of 7 degrees It will be helpful. In this book, you can get a glimpse of ad lib playing with tremendous momentum while crossing both hands of Cecil Taylor. Overall, I think it's a medium-level or higher difficulty book, but it's a great textbook for anyone who wants a higher level pianist.

『McCoy Tyner:Jazz Piano Playing』(Aki Takase / Rittor Music)1979

McCoyTyner's performance is different from Be-Bop's performance, with the left hand "floating chord" (fourth chord) and right hand pentatonic, centered on the mode. This book contains songs from early "inception" and culminating "Super Trio". A powerful and speedy performance is just like the name of a great master. It's difficult for beginners to play, but it's a valuable resource for everyone who plays jazz piano.

『Chick Corea:Jazz Piano Playang』(Makoto Terashita/ Rittor Music)1979

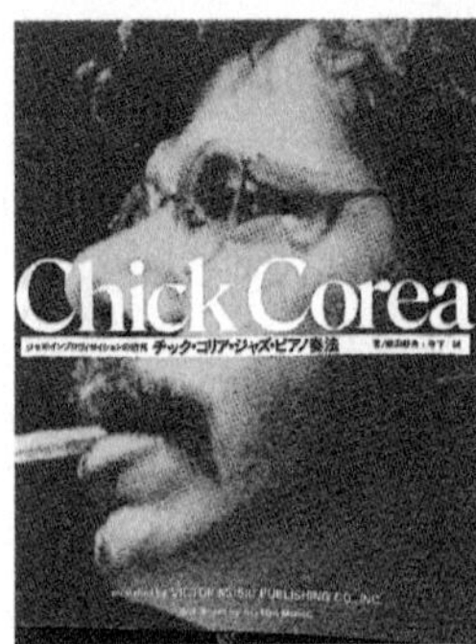

It features all the representative songs from Chick Korea's important album. The title song from "Now He Sings Now He Sobs" that feels a new generation of piano trio, the beautiful song "Noon Song", "Ballad" from the representative album "Piano Improvisations.vol.1" of the solo piano boom in the 70s for Anna ".

"Sometime Ago" from "Return to forever", representing 70s jazz. "La Fiesta" is now a standard jazz song. Recently, "Spain", which is often covered, is also posted. This is a useful textbook for learning new jazz after Be-Bop, such as progressive phrases, poly chords, $\frac{6}{8}$, or $\frac{3}{4}$ time signatures.

『Winton Kelly:Jazz Piano Playing』(Aki Takase/ Rittor Music)1979

Speaking of Winton Kelly, it can be said that it is the royal road of the modern jazz piano. Therefore, this book is a great teaching material for those who play jazz piano.

In particular, "Dead leaves" and "On a clear day" are great learning materials for first-time learners, so I recommend playing them.

『The Study Of Cross Over Keybordist Series Vol.1 : Joe Sample』
『The Same Title Vol.2 Dave Grusin』
『The Same Title Vol.3.Richard Tee』
（Tomoyuki Hayashi ／Rittor Music）1979〜82

I don't think I've heard the name crossover recently.
In my memory, the fusion of jazz and rock had already been called "jazz rock" in the 1960s. In the 70s, I think it changed to "Black Funk" → "Crossover" → "Fusion".
Anyway, even if you can play 4 beat jazz, you can't always play fusion 16 beat music. It is difficult to perform unless you are used to the rhythm. In this respect, the feature of this book can be grasped from the performances of the three keyboard players who received the most attention at that time.
Speaking of Joe Sample, "Melody of Love" is melodic and its lyrical performance is wonderful. I personally like Joe Sample the best of the three.
Dave Grusin has the impression of being an intelligent and delicate pianist. Rhythm patterns using left and right combinations are now examples of fusion piano playing.
Richard Tee has a powerful and rhythmic performance, but "Let's go by A train" is a good idea. A strong gospel performance with a slightly longer intro, but with the left hand octave alternately. I was amazed at how to play jazz super famous standards like this. Anyway, this book is very valuable because it seems to be the first fusion keyboard textbook in Japan.

『Contemporary Keybord Chord Work』（Tomoyuki Hayashi / Rittor Music）1979

The author, Tomoyuki Hayashi has written many textbooks, of these is a very good textbook. It can be said that it is for first learners because it starts with the pitch and the Chord, but it is easy to understand overall. For example, the explanation of substitute chords is explained by the relationship from relatives that are naturally explained in classical harmony (although it is often omitted in jazz theory books). Then, it is easy to understand that the chorde work of "A-form" and "B-form" including the familiar tension in John Megan's textbook is explained in the relationship between "same key" and "same key minor". Furthermore, the Comping pattern is not 4 beat jazz, but the fusion style that was popular at the time of publication of this book is a feature not found in other jazz theory books. It is also good that this book has a sonosheet.

『How to Play Improvisation For Jazz PianoVol.1』 『The Same titleVol.2』（Sadayasu Fujii/ Rittor Music）1979

Jazz standard songs are C, F, Bb, Eb for major keys, Am, Dm, GmCm for minor keys. In other words, most of the keys are flat. Therefore, textbooks are often learned with these keys. However, even if it is a C major key, proxy chords and modulation can be freely performed, so if you learn with 12 keys as in this book, the range of performance will be improved accordingly.

Volume 1 is "Chord", "Arpeggio of chord including tension", scale practice (Ionian scale, Dorian scale, AlteredDominant 7th Scale, etc.), various chord progressions

(Volumes such as I-VIm7-IIm7-V7-I, I- bIIIdim-IIm7-V7-I, etc.), variations with various chord patterns, etc. There are also practice of sequence patterns and parallel phrases, so it will be very helpful for progressive performance.

However, only the right hand is available for both Volume 1 and Volume 2. The left hand may not have been posted because there is no change as much as the right hand, but However, I wanted the left hand Voicing to be posted.

『JAZZ PIANO CHORD WORK』（Sadayasu Fujii / Rittor Music） 1979

The contents of this book are similar to Don Haerle's "JAZZ / ROCK VOISINGS for the CONTEMPORARY KEYBOARD PLAYER". Perhaps this book was based on that book.
As with Don Haerle's book, left-hand Voicing and two-hand Voicing are well documented.
Modal codework is more detailed than Don Haerle's book.

『JAZZ PIANO MODE STUDY（Sadayasu Fujii /Rittor Music） 1979

This is the first jazz piano textbook specializing in mode playing in Japan. Features of each mode, harmonization, and adlib examples of Cannonball Adderley, John Coltrane, Herbie Hancock, McCoy Tyner, Stanley Talentine are also posted. I think you can get a general sense of what mode jazz is about. However, I think that there are many places where this textbook can be helpful, considering that each player plays in their own way. For the performance of the mode, the chapters "SEQUENCE" and "PARALLEL" in the book "Jazz Piano Improvisation Technique 2" written by Sadayasu Fujii will be helpful.

『Jazz Improvisation Series : Piano 』（Dominic Spera, Japanese Translation by Masaru Uchibori/Nichion）1980

Author Dominic Spera has co-starred with trumpeter, composers / arrangers, Bart Bacharach, Petra Clarke, Johnny Mathis, Andy Williams, Henry Mancini. The contents of this book are based on explanations of basic codes and scales used in blues. Furthermore, the 9th and 13th sounds are called color tones, and the chords containing these sounds are called color codes. . Also, the accompanying phrases are simple, so it is easy to play. In the second half, the blues including the proxy code is called New Blues, and the exercise continues. There are no special esoteric codes or phrases, so it is recommended for beginners.

『Modal & Contemporary Patterns』 (David N. Baker/ Charles Colin; Treble Clef Edition edition)1980

Author DAVID BAKER is a composer and trombone player. He has written many textbooks. Producer and engineer DAVID BAKER is a different person. This book is a progressive ad-lib textbook with a focus on modal performance. The modal approach has the advantage of being able to play freely, without being bound by the master-slave relationship between the sound and the central tone, like the major and minor scales. In this book, all musical scales and diminished scales are classified as modal patterns in addition to Dorian mode, which is often used in jazz, as modal patterns. In dominant motion, modal interpretation is based on pentatonic. I also covered Coltrane's "Countdown" and "Giant Steps", but this song is not directly related to mode, but it is a progressive way of interpreting chord progressions, playing in pentatonic, and so on. Is shown. Coltrane, after releasing this song, developed it into a mode-like song, and I was convinced that he eventually went on the road to free jazz.

『Boogie Woogie Hanon 』(Leo Alfassy Amsco Publications) 1980

Boogie Woogie Piano is a classic jazz piano. Jazz piano learners don't have to play Boogie Woogie Piano just as classical piano scholars learn Bach's inventions, Hanon and Tzerny. However, I feel very happy playing Boogie Woogie Piano. By the way, Roland Hana and others in modern jazz have adopted the Boogie Woogie Piano style, and I think practicing Boogie will be quick to play fusion styles such as Richard Tea. This is because the role of the left hand is more important than the modern jazz piano in the piano style before modern jazz, so it helps to improve the technology. The Leo Alfassy Hanon Series includes Jazz Hanon and Blues Hanon.

『Transcribed voicings』(Jamey Aebersold/ Jame Aebersold)1980

Comping textbook. Comping textbook. I think the number of sounds is much higher than the actual performance because of the textbook.

Neither song is shown as an example of camping with specific music as an example. In the first half, examples of comping are shown for each chord, and in the second half, comping in blues and dominant 7th comping in the 4th degree are shown. Generally speaking, there are many parallel voicing movements. Although it will be an improvement in technology, it may be bored because it can be said that it is a mechanic training book in short

『NUNES』 Steve Doherty,Warren Nunes/Hansen house)1981

There are 31 exercises in all.

A book of be-bop style ad-lib practice with basic chord progression, dominant motion (II-V) based on a diatonic scale. There is no explanation like Dorian, Mixolidia, or Altard. However, there are exercises such as diminished, whole scale, natural minor scale, harmony minor scale melodic minor scale. It is easy to understand where the approach notes for ad-lib are properly explained. It may be a good idea for first learners to start with a textbook like this. As another feature, a camping score is posted in parallel with the ad lib score, so the score is three-tiered.

『OSCAR PETERSON JAZZ PIANO SOLOS』(Kayo Mstunobe/Nichion)1981

I think Oscar Peterson has a lot of Trnscriptions, but this book is a very good textbook, especially because it covers the best performances at the peak.

The songs are "NIGHT TRAIN", "C JAM BLUES", "GEORGIA ON MY MIND", "BAG'S GROOVE", "I Got It Bad And That Ain't Good", "PerdidoBody And Soul", "Who Can I Turn" To "," Take The 'A' Train "," TRISTEZA "When I was watching TV, a genius jazz pianist, a younger elementary school boy, came out and played "Let's go on the Take the A train". The surroundings applauded. Actually, this book P65-71 was played as it was, and it was neither improvisation nor anything.

『JAZZ PIANO FAN』 (Masaru Imada /YAMAHA MUSIC FOUNDATION) 1981

I don't know how many volumes of this "JAZZ PIANO FAN" series, but the textbook written by Masaru Imada is probably only this book, so it may be a valuable textbook in that sense.

9 songs included in the standard songs "I CAN'S GET STARTED", "I FALL IN LOVE TOO EASILY", "POLKA DOTS AND MOONBEAMS" "I THOUGHT ABOUT YOU", "MY ONE AND ONLY LOVE" "LEFT ALONE" Masaru Imada's original songs "LITTLE BLUE", "3 × 3 STEPS", "PIKO", the difficulty level is between beginner and intermediate. Those who can play jazz piano will be good to play as the next step up.

『IMPROVISING & ARRENGING ON THE KEYBOARD』 (James Oesterich, Earl Pennington/Prentige-Hall ING.) 1981

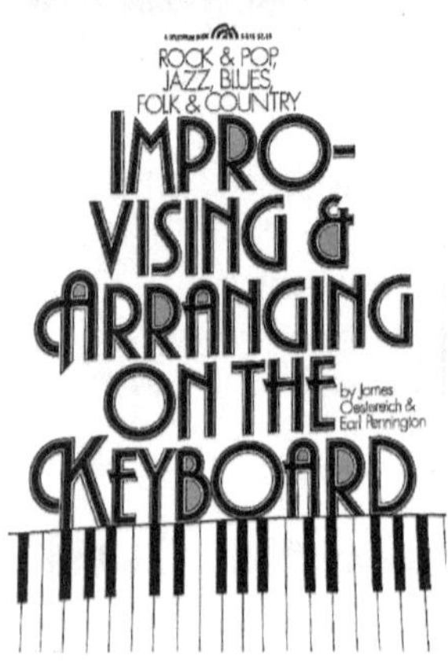

It is a textbook for beginners, since it starts with the pitch and provides basic explanations such as chords and scales. It also describes how to play not only Jazz but Folk, County music, Rock.

What is characteristic is that 40 pages of Modal jazz are explained. For the mode playing method, "Non Diatonic tones" (non-diatonic approach), "Cromatic Passing Chord" (example of chromatic chord usage), "The Suspended forth" (example of chord usage by Sus4) etc. are written . The book is worth reading because they are not detailed in other textbooks. The pentatonic is not written.

『JAZZ VOCAL REPERTORY VOL.1 』(Kotani Astuo、Shigeru Maruyama /TOSHIBA EMI MUSIC/ Rittor Music) 1982

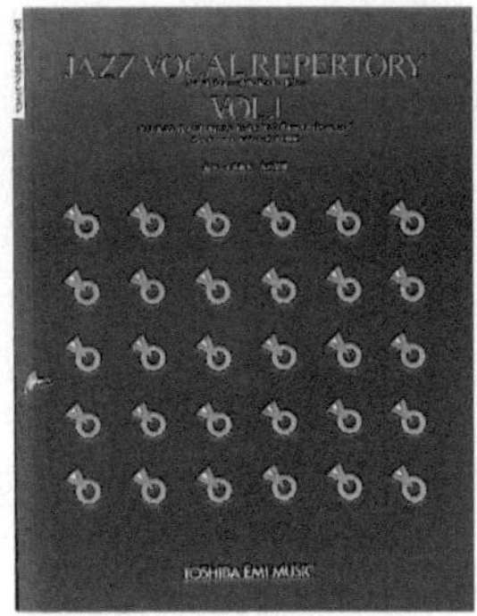

Was there a jazz vocal and jazz piano textbook before this book was published? I think this book was probably the first in Japan to be a textbook that imagined music with jazz vocals and piano. Jazz vocals rarely sing music score exactly like pop music. That's why pianists need flexibility. In other words, while comping helps vocals, he may lead vocals. And since the vocalist's range is diverse, you may need a technique that can play any key if possible. In this sense, this book will help you expand your pianist and improve your performance.

『JAZZ SOUNDS PIANO SOLO』(YuzuruSera、Tomoyuki Hayashi/ Rittor Music) 1982

This series has up to three volumes.
All are mainly ballad performances, and there are no styles such as walking bass line on the left hand and ad lib on the right hand, so the difficulty level is between elementary and intermediate. It's not that difficult, so it might be just right to increase your repertoire.

『Jazz piano Adlib Master』(Atsuo Kotani/ Rittor Music) 1982

"On Green Dolphin Street", "Autum leaves", "Blues", "Misty" are posted. Explanations of chords, scale, approach notes, etc. required to play these songs , And ad-lib examples.
It is not necessarily for beginners because it is not a textbook that explains from the pitch, but the explanation of one song and one song is polite, so it is a good textbook to work on carefully.
The first edition has a sonoseat, and subsequent revisions have a CD.

『Inside the Score: A Detailed Analysis of 8 Classic Jazz Ensemble Charts』(Rayburn Wright / Kendor Music)1982

I think this was a textbook that was highly appreciated by composers and arrangers when it was released. In addition to just posting scores, SAMMY NESTICO, THAD JONES, BOBBROOKMEYER songs are explained by picking up Melody, Vocsing, Passing Chord, substitute chords, each part section, ensemble features, etc. There are also interviews for each composer. I think this is a great book for those who are trying Big Band arrangements.

『Virtuoso Jazz Stylings-an Introduction-Intermediate Piano』

You can learn how to play BLUSE, DIXELAND, SWING, BEBOP style. It looks like a pretty gorgeous version, but it's as thin as 64 pages. The arrangement is clear and easy to understand. It is an affordable textbook for those who want to learn solo piano, and can be recommended for beginners.

『Akira Inoue Arrange Seminar』(Akira Inoue/Rittor Music) 1982

Akira Inoue is an active composer and arranger, but this book explores what arrangement is from various angles. Roughly introducing the contents, the basic edition: Melody, Harmony, Harmony, progression,
Instrument edition: About the instrument, About the effector, Practice edition: As the actual arrangement, the Beatles "Get Back" is rock and roll, fusion, ballad, It is trying in various styles such as New Wave, Stiby Wonder, Enka, and how to establish the originality of the studio work arranger. With a sonosheet, you can get a glimpse of the recording scenery in the actual studio. This is a very interesting textbook.

『Toshiko Akiyoshi Best Collect』(Toshiko kiyoshi / Rittor Music) 1983

Speaking of Toshiko Akiyoshi, I can most imagine the activities of the big band led by himself. Being an orchestra that played only Toshiko Akiyoshi's original songs was a breakthrough, and it was the biggest band in the world. Musically, there are "Insights" on the theme of Minamata disease, "Solitaire" on the theme of Ensign Onoda, and an album on the theme of the atomic bomb in Hiroshima, and she feels like a socialist musician. It is. This book is a songbook and may not be directly related to the activities of the big band, but it still makes Toshiko Akiyoshi's music feel deep. It is a valuable asset in music history, not jazz history.

『JAZZ HARMONY STEP1、2』(Toshihiko Iida/Zenon) 1983

Iida Jazz School's principal, Toshihiko Iida's book, probably used in schools, but there are volumes 1 and 2. Each is divided into theory and practice.
The first volume starts with a pitch, and includes basics such as "chord name", "diatonic scale" and "diatonic chord", "cadence", "rehabilitation", "dominant motion", "second lead minant", etc. You can learn a great jazz theory. The practice book is about Voicing, a piano keyboard. It is divided into Afom and Bform, which are familiar in John Megan's textbook. " Days of Wine and Roses" is published as an example song.
The second volume is "Minor chords and scales", "Transposition", "Rotation conversion", "Fraction chords", "Diminished chords", "Chord tones, non-chord tones", various "Harmonization" etc. It shows how to make an "ad lib phrase" as a practical skill. Both volumes 1 and 2 are in a workbook style where you learn while writing the answers to the tasks.

『CHICK COREA』(Chick Corea Children's Songs For Piano Solo/Zenon) 1983

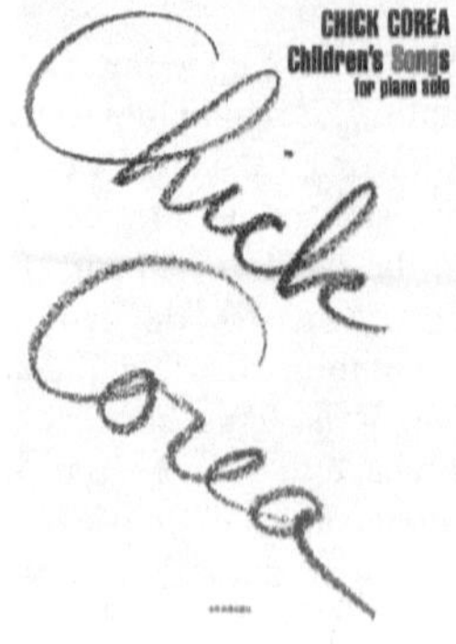

Speaking of children's songs, I think of a jazz version of Bartok's microcosmos, but this book is not specifically written for children to play. (It's not a difficult song, so it's OK for children to play.) Japanese artist Taro Okamoto often said that children's drawings were the best. That is, he did not tell children, but told adults not to forget the pure feelings of a child. This song collection may have been composed with such feelings. The song is characterized by a flowing ostinato throughout, but it is a collection of well-sensed works that feel both comfortable and powerful.

『Keybord Study』(Norio Maeda、ABO MUSIC Keybord Society /OngakunoTomosya)1983

A total of 12 volumes. If you briefly introduce each volume, Vol.1 "How the cord works", Vol.2 "How the cord works", Vol.3 "Assembling harmony", Vol.3 "Scale and tension", Vol.4 "Various chord progressions" Vol. 5 "", Vol. 6 "How to transpose and handle chords", Vol. 7 "Close voicing", Vol. 8 "Open voicing", Vol. 9 "Utilities of lines and chords" Vol.10 "Keyboards and arrangements", Vol.11 "Popular style" Vol.12 "Jazz style".
I will skip the detailed explanation of each volume, but it is such a large book that I can learn most of jazz and popular piano. But now, there is no theory that can only be learned in this textbook. However, what is newer than the previous textbooks is that there are exercises on fusion keyboards such as Joe Sample and Dave Grusin, and the playing style of Keith Jarrett.

『JAZZ PIANO SEMINOR』(Kzuo Nobuta/Shinko Music) 1983

Very good book. The transcripition songs are "ON GREEN DOLPHIN STREET" (WYNTON KELLY) "C JAM BLUES", (RED GARLAND),"BLUES ETUDE" (OSCARPETERSON), "TWO LOVES" (DUKE JORDAN), "SOL EYES" (McCOY TYNER), "NEVER" (WYNTON KELLY), "ON A CLEAR DAY" (BILL EVANS), etc.
Each chord, scale, surrogate chord, approach note, etc. are explained in detail. If you learn in this book, it will be quite powerful.

『The Jazz Composition of John Coates,JR』(Jr. John Coates, Bill Dobbins / Shawnee Press)1983

When I listened to John Coates Jr.'s music, I immediately thought that his country-inspired music sounded like Keith Jarrett. However, it seems that Keith Jarrett was playing drums with John Coates Junior band. It may be better to say that Keith was influenced by John Coates Jr. Since it is a song book, there is no ad-lib publication, but it is a collection of songs with a good sense. If you want to perform like John Coates Jr., Keith Jarrett, or Georgie Winston, you should also refer to the country piano textbook.

『Introduction For Jazz Piano playing』(REMEDIA music Institute) 1984

Comping textbook.
Eight issues are set.
Drop2 nd technique (On Green Dolphin Street), Rhythm variation (Take The "A" Train), Blues basics (Now's The Time), 3-beat practice (Green Sleeves), Progressive chord application (Sonny Moon For Two) , Poly code example (Satin Doll), role of top tone (Another), general practice (Shiny Stocking).
All the published songs are famous standard songs, and you can learn the basics of comping in this book.

『Arranging Project For Today's Music』(Eiji Kitahara / Nichion) 1985 With Sonosheet

The contents of the book are "notation", "chord progression", "chord scale", "rhythm arrangement", "rhythm assembly", "arrangement composition", "horn arrangement", "strings & chorus arrangement" You can learn all sorts of things. The feature of this book is that it is writing with emphasis on rhythm arrangement unlike the arrangement textbooks published before this. The textbook is very easy to understand, including how to use strings. Recommended for beginners. In addition, it can be confirmed by sound because it has a sonosheet.

『ROOT'S MUSIC STUDY』(Shingo Sawada / Roots Music School) 1985

Since Sadayasu Fujii published jazz textbooks, many jazz textbooks have been published. At the same time, jazz popular schools such as "Roots Conservatory", "Muse Conservatory", "Mother House", "Lovely Music School", and "Pan School of Music" are born one after another. In addition, many jazz schools such as "Iida Jazz School (Studio)", "Yamaha Conservatory (formerly Nemu Conservatory)" and "Anne School of Music" were born. In the 1980s, staff training schools such as "Aoyama Recording School" and "Music Producer Training School MPI" will be born. There are good books in the textbooks published by jazz schools.

A total of 12 jazz piano correspondence textbooks issued by the Roots Conservatory (12 CDs or 12 cassettes as appendices). There should be no other gorgeous jazz / piano teaching materials, and I think this is a wonderful textbook born from the enthusiasm and efforts of the staff, including Satoshi Sawada, the director and guitarist. However, it may be difficult for first-time learners. This is because each volume is divided into the first half of the theory and the second half from the practical skill, so it seems difficult to understand the connection between the theory and practical skill. So when you receive these 12 volumes, do you really want to play jazz? Or do you find it difficult to play jazz? By the way, this textbook still seems to be sold on the site of the Roots Conservatory, but I was lucky enough to get this expensive textbook at Yahoo auction. When it arrived, the cassette was in a plastic bag and unopened. Perhaps this owner bought the material but did not use it. Correspondence learning is not compulsory by anyone, so a strong will is necessary to continue.

『Arranging Comcepts 』(Dick Grove/Alfred Publishing) 1985

Author Dick Grove is the founder of Dick Grove School of Music. By the way, this school is famous as a popular music school, as it is called Berklee College of Music in the East and Dick Grove in the West. Many jazz musicians, Michael Jackson and Barry Manilow also learned from the school.This book is a large book of 433 pages. Briefly, it consists of four PARTs. Part1 is instrumental method and notation, Psrt2 is Melody lighting, Voiceleading such as Common Tones, Parallel Motion, Contrary Motion, Pssing Chord pedal point and transposition, etc. Zation. Part 4 includes Dick Grove's own song "SCUFFLE" as an example. Anyway it is a very good textbook.

『Msa Mtsud's Music course : Basic knowledge of popular arrangements』 1986

l though Matsuda Masaru is famous as an electone player, this book seems to have been written for an electone player, but the contents are Jazz theory books. It does not have the unique features of this book compared to other textbooks, but since it starts with the pitch and scale, it is for first-time learners, and it has detailed explanations of chord progression, substitute chords, etc. In addition, it is very good because there are many exercises. In some places, the dialogue with the students makes the contents easy to understand. For example, the following is written. Hanako "Masa, do you all need to remember this?", Masaru says"You must remember!", Hanako says "There are six types of dominant seventh scales. Do you also need to learn 6 x 12 = 72? , Masaru Says"You must remember", Hanako sayas "I take a year to remember this all.", Masaru says"But you must remember. The diversity of dominant sevens is the appeal of jazz and popular. This is one of the major points when arranging and ad-lib. "

『MODERN JAZZ PAINO A Study in Harmony and Improvisation 』 (BrainWaite / Wise Publications) 1987

It starts with a description of the pitch, so I think it's a textbook for beginners, but it explains the chords and scales necessary for jazz performance. The first half is the codebook.

In the latter half of the book, there are a number of songs that describe only the chord symbols in how the chords are used in specific songs, but they lack specificity.In short, it's an incomplete textbook.

『Charlie Parker for Piano, Book 1』 (Paul Smith, Morris Feldman Arrangiment/ Atlantic Music) 1987

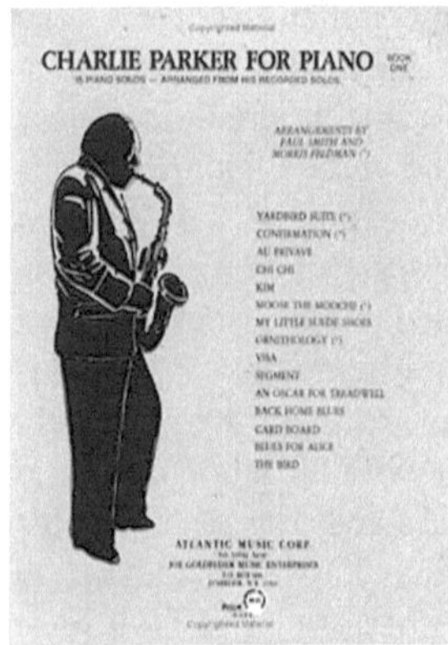

Collection of piano arrangements of songs by Charlie Parker. Because it is a Transcription from Parker's album, the ad lib is faithfully reproduced. Published songs include "AUPRIVAVE", "BACK HOME BLUSE", "THE BIRD", "CONFIRMATION" and "YARDBIRD SUITE". It is often said that Bud Powell and others replaced Parker's music with piano, but this textbook is a piano arrangement of Parker's performance itself, so there is a sense of presence. Speaking of which, a group called "Super Saxophone" arranged Parker's ad lib for five saxophones and got attention.

Parker's ad-lib can be said to be more artistic. It will be very helpful for learners.

『1000 KEYBORD IDEAS 』(Ronald Herder/Alfred Music)1987

I don't know if it is a textbook that brings 1000 ideas like the title, but the whole is composed of 11 Sctions, showing not only jazz and popular music but also various piano playing techniques such as Brahms, Bartok, Chopin, Scriabin etc. Is.
However, it does not show how to play black music such as R & B, soul, funk, or fusion.
Such a book might be useful if you have one as a piano playing dictionary.

『The Contemporary Keyboardist』 (John Novello/Warner Brothers Publications)1987

Everal revisions have been issued, but this is from 1987.
It may be a bit difficult for beginners, but it is a very good textbook. In the first half, the basic harmony, Bebop and Coltrane's "Giant Step" ad lib are explained, but the main feature of this book is a detailed explanation of the harmony. , "Secondary Dominant", "V7 of V to V7 of I" progression, surrogate chord, "Upper Strunture", "Cluster" and so on. For example, "Cluster" refers to each cluster of "3, 4, 5, 6".

Jazz rarely uses the basic chords. We often stack a number of superimposed chords with tension on top of the basic chords. This makes it possible to express complex and sophisticated music by blurring the relationship between chords. I think that if the relationship between sound and sound is completely relativized, we will move toward free jazz, but this book could be said to be a textbook just before that.

『Modal Jazz』 (Bill Dobbins/ADVANCE MUSIC) 1988

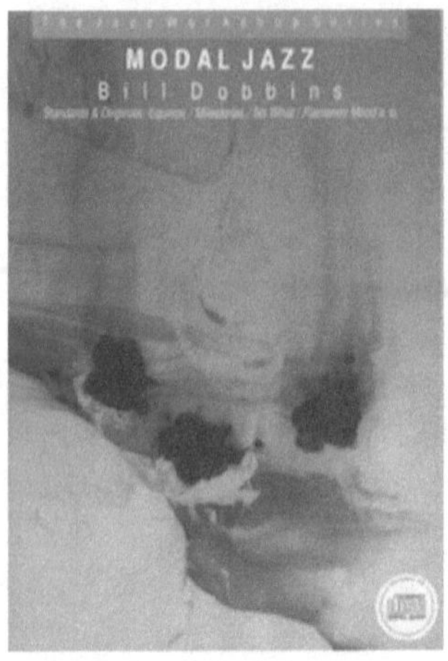

Author Bill Dobbins wrote an excellent textbook, such as "The Contemporary Jazz Pianist," which was introduced in this book.

This book is a bilingual edition written in English, French and German. How jazz is performed using Miles Davis's "So What", "Milestones", John Coltrane's "Equinox", and Dobbins' own "Flamenco Mood", "Prism", and "Spring Song". Is being analyzed. In the case of the mode, if the functional code used in the major and minor key is added easily, the characteristic of the mode may be impaired. For example, in D-Dorian mode, you often see Dm only in the first measure, and then see the score without the chord. In this case, Dm thinks that the first note of D-Dorian mode is conveniently chorded. Dobbins interprets it that way in "So what." Also, John Coltrane's "Equinox" uses C # m7, F # m7, the 4th chord, A7 # 11 and G # 7b9.

『Jazz Piano Live (Piano Solo Collection)』 (Naoki Nishi/Nchion) 1988

Published songs include "Sunrise", "The Gentle Rain", "Alone Together", "Embraceable", "Someone To Watch Over Me" and "You'd Be So Nice To Come Home to"

As for the arrangement, for example, the code etc. is almost up to 7th and simple (it may be better to say that there is no waste). Therefore, technically, I think that we can play around the end of Bayer.Anyway, the basic points necessary to play the jazz piano, that is, the jazz rhythm, and the points to acquire basic skills are held down, so I think that it is a very good textbook for beginners.

『New York Style Jazz Piano Vo1 & 2』（Kuni Mikami/Zenon）1988,1994

The author, Kuni Mikami, is a jazz pianist based in New York who studied with Barry Harris.This book introduces BarryHarris methods. Introducing the contents, the first volume (left) is the various types and applications of "Diatonic scale chords" and their application to songs. Diminished code and diminished scale, ending. 6th code (Barry Harris thinks IIm7 code is IV6 inversion, V6 is VIbm6) and its application. Examples of ad lib based on scale. The second volume (right) shows what chords should be added to the melody. Examples of performance based on the dominant 7th, minor 7th, and minor tonic 7th are "Over The Rainbow", "Santa Claus Is Coming to Town "," The More I see you "and so on. Although there are few ad-lib exercises as a whole, this book gives many hints on Voicing.

『The Jazz Piano』 (Mark Levine/ Sher Music)1989

I think that it is a well-known jazz piano textbook, but if you introduce the contents roughly, it will be entered from the description of the pitch, and "Just Friends" is used as an example to mention basic chord progression and harmonization. From P41 to P58, it is mainly written about Voicing on the left hand. P59 to P96 are explanations of scales often used in jazz. From P97 to P136, "So What Chords", "Upper Structures", "Pentatonic Scales" and explanations of techniques often used in progressive jazz. Advanced voicing usage examples from P137 to P154 (Natran of Coltrane, etc.), P155 to P166 follow "Stride and Bud Powell voicing", and "Four–Note Scales" from P167 to P178. And I think that the most enriched in this book is "Block Chords" on P179-P206. Various types of examples such as "Four-way Close", "Passing Diminish", "Drop2" and "minor Drop2 including Alt" are shown. After that, "Salsa and Latin Jazz", "Comping" etc. are explained. Even if it is written from the pitch, it is not like a training book, so it seems difficult for first-time learners to use it. I think it is for people who can play jazz piano. In short, it can be said that it is a dictionary for playing jazz piano.

『Creative-Jazz-Improvisation』(SCOTT D.REEVES/Prentic Hall)

A textbook that shows how to do ad lib, but it is very well done. The whole is composed of 19 chapters. For example, Chapter 1 "Major Scale" is Louis Armstrong's "HotterThan That", Chapter 2 "Dorian mode" is Miles Davis's "So What", Chapter 4 "II-V-I". "Progressiton" is Clifford Brown's "Pent-Up House" Chapter 6 "Lydian and Phrygian Mode" is Wayne Shorter "Masqualero", Chapter 10 "Harmonic Structures and Coltran, e Substitutions" is John Coltrane "Giant Steps", Chapter 11 "Sectional Forms and Rhythm Changes" is Charlie Parker's "Shaw 'Nuff" and Chapter 13 "Whole-Tone Scales" is Thelonious Monk's "Evidence". An example is detailed. It will be very helpful for players.

『Elements of the Jazz Language for the Developing Improvisor 』(Jerry Coker/Schaum Pubns)1991

Speaking of Jerry Coker, the book "Improvising Jazz" was translated into Japanese in the 1960s and was a musician known in Japan, but this book is a practical guide to adlib.

There are many adlib examples of famous jazz musicians. Roughly speaking, there are quite a few such as Chick Corea, Freddie Habbard, Hank Mobkey, Fats Navzrro, McCoy Tyner, Miles Davis, JimHall, J.J.Johnson, John Coltrane, Bill Evans, Blue Mitchell, Lee Morgan, Kenny Dorham, John Scofield. However, since it is called Elements, all are a few measures. (Clifford Brown and Michael Brecker's ad lib is a whole song), but with two CDs, it's a useful educational material.

『A Chromatic Approach to Jazz Harmony and Melody』 (David Liebman/Advance Music) 1991

Chromatic approach has been a very important technique since modern jazz. In the case of bebop, it could be said that it was a joint that smoothly developed phrases and phrases, chords and chords, but for more progressive jazz, the chromatic approach blurred the master-slave relationship of the whole music, It can be said that it is a method of relativizing the relationship between sound and sound. It can be said that it is similar to the flow of modern music in classical music. This book is not only jazz musicians such as McCoy Tyner, Herbie Hancock, Chick Corea, Miles Davis, John Coltrane, but also Bach, Chopin, Ives, Schoenberg, Scriabin and others. Harmonization including clusters in chromatic lines, and re-harmonization in standards. Author Leveman also mentions his work.

『Jazz Piano Light Intelligence Piano Score : Tasturo Yamashita Work1999 』 『The SameTitle :Mariya Takeuchi 』(Junichi Kamiyama /Kawai Publishing) 1992

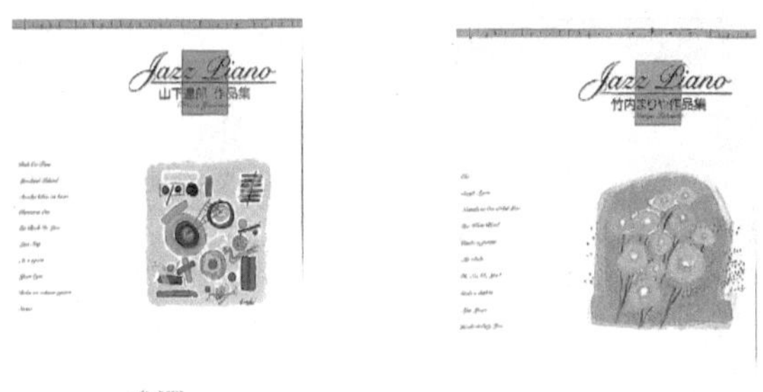

Tatsuro Yamashita, Mariya Takeuchi, Kazumasa Oda, Yumi Matsutoya, Yosui Inoue,
etc. A series of songs that play jazz on pop singer songs. It's easy to think that these kinds of songs are a little jazz-style arrangements, but these songs (see Tatsuro Yamashita and Mariya Takeuchi) are full-fledged jazz-arranged songs And it is quite difficult to play. This series is arranged by Junichi Kamiyama, and a related CD of the same name is sold by Victor. Performed by "Tim Harden Trio" (although it is a fictional name, actually played by Haruki Mino). By the way, who buys a songbook like this? Does Tatsuro Yamashita's fans buy a jazz piano, a collection of songs that are a bit difficult to play? Will the jazz pianist make the songs of Tatsuro Yamashita or Mariya Takeuchi a repertoire

『Keith Jarrett：The Koln Concert For Piano』(Keith Jarrett/Japan Schott) 1991

Keith Jarrett's solo piano became a big topic not only in the jazz world but also in the classical world from the 70s to the 80s. It is no wonder that this book was published by Schott publisher. However, because it was evaluated by the world of classical music, it does not mean that Keith's piano performance is excellent, and it does not mean that classical and jazz were inspired by each other, or that excessive meaning was laid. In short, Everyone just want to listen to Keith's piano. If possible, it would have made me want to play this kind of performance. However, as Keith mentioned in the introduction of this book, it is impossible to accurately improvise an improvisation, and the score is just a reference. Even so, the fantastic song at the beginning of this textbook is amazing. Personally, I like Keith's country-style comfortable performance. Of course, such performances are also fully published.

『JAZZ PIANO WORK SHOP：BOP STUDY』(Kzuyuki Isono/) 1992

This book consists of a book of B-Bop style, "Structure of cyclic form", "Voicing", "Backing technique", "Phrase study", and "Score examples".
Included songs are "Moose The Mooche", "Cheers", "Dexterity", "Anthropology", "Kim", "Bird's Nest", "Oleo", etc.
For the piano, there are examples of typical bebop ad-libs, including bass lines, so the basics of ad-lib performance may be a good textbook to learn.

『Masahiko Sato Piano Works』(Masahiko Sato/Zenon）1993

Masahiko Satois is a very good pianist.
He says"improvisation has no method. Although in the field of what is called Jazz they had commoly traces harmonies of the melody lines,we habe recently begun to try various kind of improvisation in such a way that we play variations by repeating our most favorite part (as many bars as we like) as many times as we like; or add a totally new element. Find your own way of enjoying music based on my book. "In other words, this work collection is more of Masahiko Sato music than jazz. However, you may feel that you need a high degree of musical skills and long experience to be able to play like him. Music is a language acquisition. However, according to an old debate about whether human abilities are innate or empirical, as Taro Okamoto often said, "Children's drawings are the best," improvisation involves an unconscious body before ecliture. There is also the aspect of driving expression. Therefore, free improvisation is for a musician with a high level of skill and background, and at the same time has the ambiguity of being open to anyone.

『Easy Jazz Piano 』(Naoki Nishi/Shinko Music）1993

"Take the A train ", "Satin Doll", "On Green Dolphin Street" or more, three standard songs played at each stage, faithfully following the melody, fake, ad-lib, It explains that jazz can be played step by step.
Although the description of harmonization is kept to a minimum, it details how to fake and adlib scale.
In the second half, "Theory and Practice Based on It," it is very good that the way of making phrases is described in detail. This is a textbook I would recommend.

『Jazz PianoSwinging Selection（Piano Solo)』（Shiori Aoyama etc/Doremi Music Publishing ）1995

The first half of this book is a collection of songs based on jazz standards, such as "Round Midnight", "Let's Go by Train A", and "Satin Doll".

A feature not found in the other collections is the Transcription of Dave Grusin, Harry Connick Jr., David Foster and Dr. John in the latter half. I don't know why this lineup was made, but it's interesting.

In particular, Dr. John's album includes Thelonious Monk's `` Blue Monk '', but there is no R & B or gospes style performance in other music collections, so I would like you to listen to the album along with the score .

『Modal Jazz Composition & Harmony Vol. 2 』（Ron Miller/ Advance Music) 1999、2002

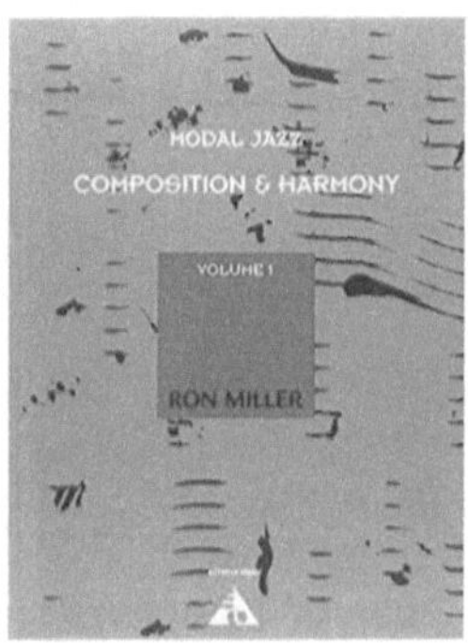

From the title's point of view, it feels like harmonization of mode jazz, but the content should be described as a textbook of "Re-Harmonyzation". Or perhaps it's the harmonization of the extended "Ave Iravel Note Scale". For example, Alterd Scale is usually used for Dominant7th, but it is also used here for Dm7th. Because the constituent notes of the Alterd Scale are the same as the melodic minor scale, the codes D, E $\flat$, F, and A hold if you consider the minor key Dm7th. Then you can get codes such as minor 2nd, major 2nd, and Sus4. Vol.2 shows many examples of songs. For example, as a melody-writing technique, Joe Henderson, Ralph Towner, Joe Zabinul, McCoy Tyner, etc. are mentioned, but the most noteworthy in this book is "Re-Harmonization" as in Volume 1. Technique.

For example, the chord progression at the beginning of "Autum leaves" is generally "Cm → F7 → bB", but in this book, there are various interesting "re-harmonization" techniques such as "Dbm9 → Gb13 → Cm7".

『VOICING FOR JAZZ KEYBORD』(FRANK MANTOOTH / HalLeonardCorp)1997

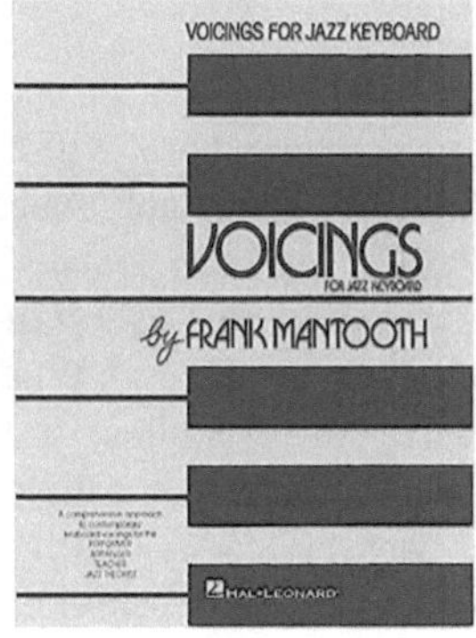

Harmonization textbook.
This book is explained by five voicing.
In particular, they have revealed the importance of four-time voicing, but they have five functions: Strong Major (3rd and 7th present), Weak Major (7th not present), Minor, Suspended Dominant (11th chords), and Lydian. Because iits is named Miracle Code. It also describes how Poly Chord and Upper structure are developed in dominant motion. It will be helpful for performing progressive performances.

『JAZZ CHORD PROGRESSIONS』(Bill Boyd / Hal Leonard Corp)1997

Something like a basic book of chords used in jazz. Most are
written in two half notes in one bar, so it feels like a collection of tasks for harmony.
It is not a practical textbook because it is not harmonized according to a specific song, but it is written assuming a frequently used chord progression, so it is useful for learning chords Would.

『JAZZ ARRANGING 』(Norman David/Scarecrow Pre ss) 1998

Speaking of JAZZ's arrangement method, it is common to start with explanations of chords and scales, and finally learn how to arrange big band from small writing methods such as 2part, 3part, 4part, etc. . This book is no exception. But today, considering that professional jazz big bands have almost disappeared, there may not be much need for direct arrangements for big bands. Nevertheless, I think there is much to learn as a basis for popular music, especially for harmonization. The feature of this book is that the writing of each section of saxophone, trumpet and trombone is written in detail, and the explanation of counter melody and octave unison for melody is easy to understand. Effective exercises are also included in each chapter.

『Jazz Standards for Piano』(Thomas Coppola/Hal Leonard Corp) 1998

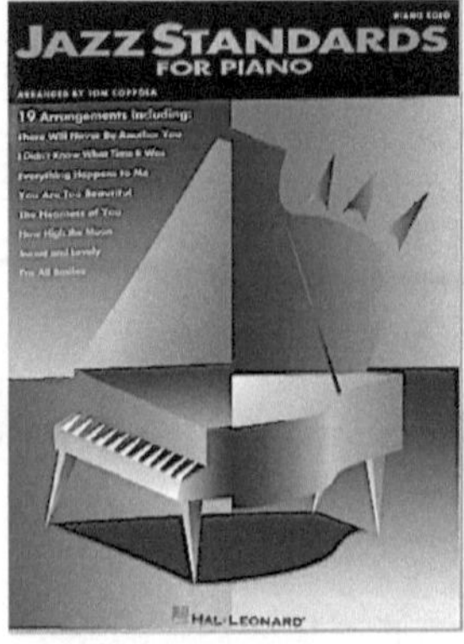

There is no ad-lib part but only the theme, but it will be a basic Chode work study. Published songs are "Alice in Wonderland", "April in Paris", "Autumn Leaves", "But Beautiful", "Everything Happens to Me", "Girl Talk", "How High the Moon", "I Didn't Know" What Time It Was, I'll Remember April, I'm All Smiles, Lush Life, The Nearness of You, People, Stella by Starlight, Sweet by Lovely, etc. By the way, the codes attached (re-harmonization and inner voice movement) are quite high-sense. I also think the "Stella by Starlight" walking baseline will be helpful to players.

『JAZZ KEYBOARD』 (NOAH BAERMAN/Alfred Pub Co)1998

A book that has been divided into three books: "Beginning" (beginner), "Intermediate" (intermediate), and "Mastering" (advanced).
"Beginning" (elementary) focuses on chords up to the 7th, simple ad-lib lines such as arpeggios and diatonic scales. "Mastering" (intermediate) includes chromatic ad libs, harmonization and comping (including salsa, bossa nova, and samba) by alternated dominants including tension,"Mastering" (advanced) focuses on modal performance, 4th voicing, substitute chords and re-harmonization, taking "So What" as an example.
Overall, it's a simple and clear textbook, so it's easy to use for first-time learners.

『Ｊａｚｚ＆Ｐｏｐ Ｔｈｅｏｒｙ Ｓｅｒｉｅ：Chord Progression (With CD)』
Eiichi Fujii ／YMM）1998

A workbook for learning chords and chord progressions. Compared to other textbooks, it is not particularly distinctive. It's a writable workbook, so it's good for organizing minor chord progressions, how to use borrowed chords, etc. It will also be a study because there are transposition tasks. It's also interesting to see in the description of the mode that it shows what happens when you apply the mode to the code normally used in Cm's Key. However, it is only four pages, so I think it would have been better to dig a little deeper. The good thing about this book is that it comes with a CD.

『Jazz & PopTheory Serie : Arrangement (With CD)』 (Takayuki Hirano/YMM) 1998

The title is a textbook in the "Jazz Pop Theory Series", but the content is more like a pop arrangement textbook than jazz. A jazz arrangement would be a harmonization-oriented textbook that assumes the arrangement of a big band, but this book starts with an arrangement of rhythm instruments.

The examples of drums and bass notation, how to assemble intros, interludes, and endings, and the latter half of the book provide detailed and easy-to-understand explanations of instrumental methods, strings, and horn section configurations.

Harmonization studies tend to be the main focus of classical and jazz composition and arrangement methods (although that is important, of course), but rhythm and timbre are more important today when PCs have become indispensable in the field of music expression. In this regard, this book is a very good textbook.

This series seems to have up to 6 volumes. To put it simply, Re-harmonization textbook with 12 standard songs. A style of learning while performing characteristic harmony for each song. For example, "The Girl from Ipanema"
(4th Interval Buiid) and "Fly Me to the Moon" (Diminish's Upper Structure Triad). Know as many techniques as possible to change the basic code of Tonic, Subdominant, and Dominant. To acquire the ability to return the reharmonized harmony to the basic code (T, SD, D). Be honest with your musical desires without being particular about tonality.

『Jazz piano Collection/Red Garlamd』 (Shiro Sato/Shinko Music) 1998

As noted in the introduction to this book, I think Red Garland is a great learning material for beginners of jazz piano. That said, Red Garland's light single tone and block chord performances are clear and easy to understand.

The "C Jam Blues" featured in several other textbooks has the same performance, but it can be said to be a model for jazz piano.

Also, "My Romance" is as good or better than Bill Evans's performance. "Will Weep For Me" is a performance that can be a model for block chords. Other performances are also wonderful. I really want you to refer to it.

『Blue Note and Tonality Basic Theory for Improvisation and Composition (with CD)』 (Motohiko Hamase/Zenon) 1998

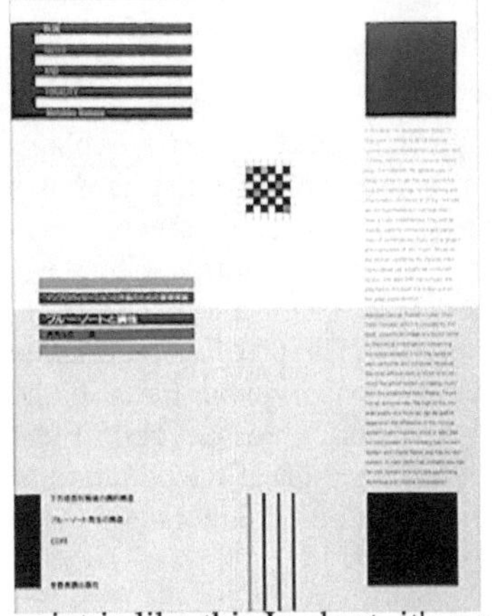

This book is about music and improvisation possibilities based on "descent overtones" .To be honest, I didn't know that there was a concept of descending harmonics before reading this book.According to the author's own words, " down harmonics "are inverse consonants, and unlike "upper harmonics", the fundamentals are not fixed and there are many fundamentals, so It becomes a multi-tone world because it becomes ambiguous, and considering the descending harmonics of the major scale, it has the potential of b3 and b7, so it is the basis for the blue note.Addition, it matches the acoustic area of Sus4. "Well, I think the main point is like this.In short, it's a great hint for progressive improvisation.In any case, this book showing its own theory that is not imitation of existing jazz theory like this book should be more appreciated.The Japanese nature that allows only certain evaluations must be revised.

『Funk And R&B Keybord Method』(Peter Gelling /KoalaPublications) 1998

It consists of three chapters and 19 lessons.
There are several types of Funk keyboard textbooks, but this is probably the most introductory level because every chapter has keyboard instructions.
Chapter 1 explains the basic chords, so if you can play jazz piano to some extent, you can skip this chapter. Chapter 2 is an exercise where the right hand combines blues scale with the left hand bass line. In Chapter 3, the 7th chord is added to the 16-beat rhythm, so it becomes difficult to play little by little. the last lesson 19 is a typical pattern lesson used in funk and R & B. It can be recommended as an introductory book that even inexperienced pianoers can play. But if you can play jazz piano to a certain extent, the following textbooks would be better.

『Funk Keyboards: The Complete Method 』(Master Class、Gail Johnson / Musicians Institute) 1999

There are eight chapters in all. Chapter 1 explains the chords using keyboard figures. Chapter 2 is a rhythm pattern without a chord. Chapter 3 is a rhythm pattern with two-handed chords, Chapter 4 is phrasing, Chapter 5 is a chromatic approach, Chapter 6 is a base pattern, Chapter 7 is a complex technique, and Chapter 8 is typical Funk piano patterns and songs. There are several Funk textbooks available, but it's a great introduction to Funk keyboards for jazz piano beginners and those who have never played jazz.

『Jazz Piano Concepts & Techniques』(John Valerio/Hal Leonard Corp 1998
『Jazz Piano Technique: Exercises, Etudes & Ideas for Building Chops』
(John Jalerio/ Hal Leonard Corp) 2013
『 How to Play Solo Jazz Piano: Chapters Include: Chords & Voicings,
Bass Lines, Swing Tunes, Ballads, Improvisation』(John Valerio Hal
Leonard Corp) 2016

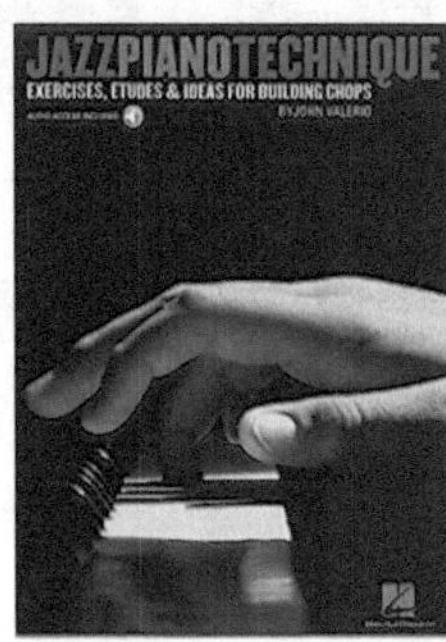

I sometimes get the question: "I want to play jazz piano, but is there any good textbook?" If you want to play jazz in earnest, going to a jazz school will be quick, but as I did, I went to a bookstore or a musical instrument store to buy a textbook and play a jazz piano. I think it would be a normal action.

As I already mentioned, when I was interested in jazz, there were a few jazz piano textbooks published, but there were few textbooks that could be used by first learners. In that respect, a large number of textbooks have been published. However, because of the large number of publications, you may be wondering what to buy.

In addition, since classical music has a fixed sound in the score, the overall picture of the target music is clear and the method can be easily squeezed. But because Jazz is improvised and jazz pianist is also a composer, it is difficult to present a textbook that will be a step to satisfy such a wide range of musical skills and backgrounds. The textbooks used also differ depending on the learner's musical background. "I have never played an instrument, but I like jazz and want to play the piano." For example, "I never played jazz, but I used to play a little classical piano." I've never played a guitar or trumpet.

For the time being, I would recommend the book "Jazz Piano Concepts & Techniques" in the upper left, as long as it can be played with Bayer techniques. (Tomorrow most of the time, you might want a different textbook), but it contains chord descriptions, chord works, chords for melodies, and techniques necessary for jazz first learners. Although it is not an ad-lib learning book, it can be played enough with Bayer techniques, so I would recommend this book as the first book to those who have never played jazz. By the way, the author John Valerio has published many other textbooks. If you can play this book (you can use it together), the middle and right books are also good books, so I'd like you to challenge them.

『The World's Best Piano Arrangements』(Alfred Publishing Staff/Schaum Pubns)1999

Many pianists of the swing era are introduced. You can enjoy pianist styles such as George Shearing, Art Tatum, Teddy Wilson, Duke Ellington, Dave Brubeck, Bill Evans, Bob Zurke, Mary Lou Williams, Hazel Scott Jess Stacy, Ed Shanaphy, etc. However, the left hand is often the 10th, so Japanese people with small hands need to be creative. Also, most songs have no chord names (only Dave Brubeck and Bill Evans perform chords), which may be difficult for first-time learners. Isn't it a songbook more than an intermediate person?

『Jazz Combo Copy Series Vol.2：Tommy Flanagan』(Shinko Music) 1999

Tommy Flanagan can be said to be B-Bop's leading pianist, but also participated in some of Jazz's most famous albums, such as Sony Rollins' Saxophone Colossus and Coltrane's Giant Steps. It is also known as a good supporter.

Therefore, this book is the perfect Transcription for jazz piano learners.

Moreover, it is a piano trio performance, but I am glad that it has not only the piano but also the bass and the drum score (including the drum solo score).

『How to Play R&B Soul Keyboards』(Henry Soleh Brewer/Hal Leonard)1999

The contents are based on the shuffle pattern of the early 1950s Motown R & B, the pattern of repeating the root and 5 degrees with the left hand of the 1960s, and the synthesizers such as StevieWonder and Billy Beck in the 1970s such as Clavinet, Fender Rose Piano, Mini Moog etc. Keyboard play. Use of polyphonic synthesizers found in Prince, jimmy Jam, Leon Sylvwes, etc. in the 1980s, and a combination technique of both hands based on sixteenth notes. It covers a wide range, including those from the 1990s sampling keyboard. However, all exercises are mainly riffs of about 4 bars. For example, Motown Turnback, Chicago Turnback, 60's 4 Bar Turnback, 70's 4 Bar Turnback, R & B Turnback, Blues Turnback, Slow Blues etc. If you think of this book as a training book, it feels like it isn't. So it's a good way to get a glimpse of how black popular music piano keyboards have changed.

『A Classical Approach to Jazz Piano』(Dominic Alldis /Hal Leonard Corp) 2000

This book is a textbook of chord work.
Enter from the description of the scale and basic chords, harmony to the melody, "Reharmonization", "Four-Part Harmony", "Playing the Melody", "Five-Part Harmony", "polychords", "upper structure triads," "block chords "and" Pentatonic harmony ". The overall features are detailed in terms of inner voice movement.
This is because the title "Classical Approach" in this book does not mean a jazz classical approach, but rather a (classical music) harmony approach to modern Western music. By the way, in the classical harmony method, non-harmonic sounds are assumed to be resolved into harmony sounds, but non-harmonic sounds in jazz are often interpreted by the words tension and approach note. Moreover, the tension itself is used continuously. Therefore, this book shows that up to 7th chords can be interpreted in a classical way, but the chord work including tension is different.

With CD EiichiFuji Jazz PianoTraining ♩ (Eiichi Fujii /YMM) 2000

There are up to Part 10, but Part 1 is a short phrase practice to learn the jazz piano swing feeling. Part2 is three small practice songs. Part3 is a simple blues with six sounds. Part 4 "Ad-lib Using Chord Patterns" teaches basic jazz techniques by practicing using the Dorian Scale, Mixolydian Scale, and Altered Dominant Scale. Part 5 "Example of chord progression ad lib" is a further development of Part 4. Part 6 blues practice is a practice of adding other sounds to the 6 tone blues of Part 3. Part 7 is slow ballad playing, and Part 8 is the practice of ad-lib in the transposition. Part 9 is applied practice, and Part 10 is the practice of two songs by the author. There are plenty of variations for training, so it will be one of the best books by Eiichi Fujii.

『Osaka University of Arts, School Of Music : Correspondence Course Music Textbook』（Hiroshi Nanatsuya、KAzuo Uehara、Eiji Kitahara/ Osaka University of Arts）2001

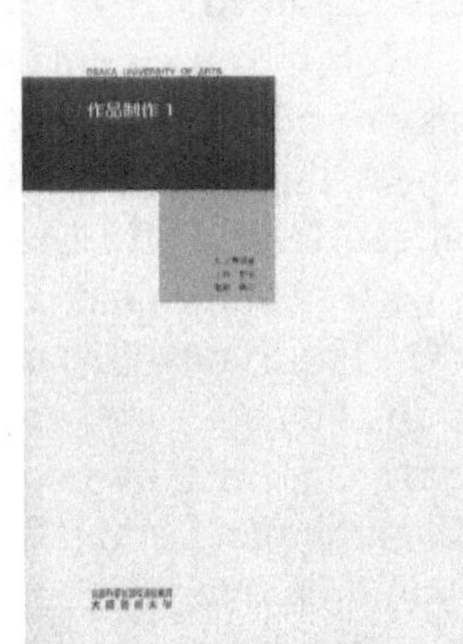

Osaka University of Arts is the only music college in Japan that has distance learning education. You can also earn a degree.

The college curriculum seems to teach composition in three fields: classical music, computer music, and popular music. Therefore, this textbook reflects that. Graduation requires going to campus, so not everything is learned online. People who want to study music at university while working, who wanted to study at a music college in the past but who have given up on high tuition, or who want to take on the challenge again, will be able to meet the needs of a variety of students.

『Jazz Piano Colection : Kenny Drew』 (Shiro Sato/Shinko Music)2001

Speaking of Kenny Drew, I remembers releasing many commercial albums at the request of a Japanese record company in his later years.

But when I ask again now, every performance is wonderful.

First of all in this book, "I Can't Get Started" is easy to play in C major. You'll also find some examples of jazz piano, such as "Drop2", "Upper Structure Triad", and "falling semitone progression".

"It Could Happen To You" has a variety of pedal points, one of Drew's features, and a 4th pitch drop, parallel phrases, etc. will enrich your performance. "Lullaby of Birdland", "Softly, As In A Morning Sunrise", and "You'd Be So Nice To Come Home To" are perfect for minor key ad-lib practice.

『Latin Jazz piano』(Fumikazu Hirata / Ritto inc) 2001

I think this is the first full-scale textbook of Latin jazz piano in Japan. Speaking of Latin jazz piano performances, it is characterized by a unique performance technique accompanied by a syncopation called Montuno. Even if you can play 4-beat jazz, it's not always easy to play because of the different styles. In this respect, this book has 98 exercises with a CD, and you can learn Latin jazz piano step by step. However, what is unfortunate is that the songs "Giant Steps", "On The Sunny Side of The Street", and "A Night in Tunisia" are not recorded on the CD for some reason. Still, it's cool to play Coltrane's "Giant Steps" with Latin jazz piano. In particular, Latin jazz piano playing has a wide range of applications, so it would be interesting to try playing your favorite music in Latin jazz piano style with reference to this textbook.

『THE PROFICIENCY VOL.1』(Hiroshi Koizumi/Self Publishing) 2001

Speaking of Hiroshi Koizumi, as a New Breed concert master, I often saw him playing the piano in the Fuji TV family competition.

It was a simple arrangement, so I could play at first glance, but it was a full-fledged jazz songbook. Anyway, the notes are big and easy to see. The songs are `` Day Of Wine And Roses '', `` Satin Doll '', `` All Of Me '', `` Over The Rainbow '', `` Smoke Gets In Your Eyes '', `` But Beautiful '', `` As Times Goes By '', `` The `` Shadow Of Your Smiles '', `` Moon River '', `` Autumn Leaves '', `` My Foolish Heart '', `` Tea For Two '', `` Fly Me To Moon '', `` Meditation '' Vo.1, but the sequel is published It doesn't seem to be.

『Jazz Piano Solos SeriesVol.1Miles Davis』(Arr by Brent Edstrom& James Sodke/Hal Leonard Corp) 2001
『The Same Title Vol.7 Smooth jazz』(Arr by Larry Moore /Hal Leonard Corp) 2001

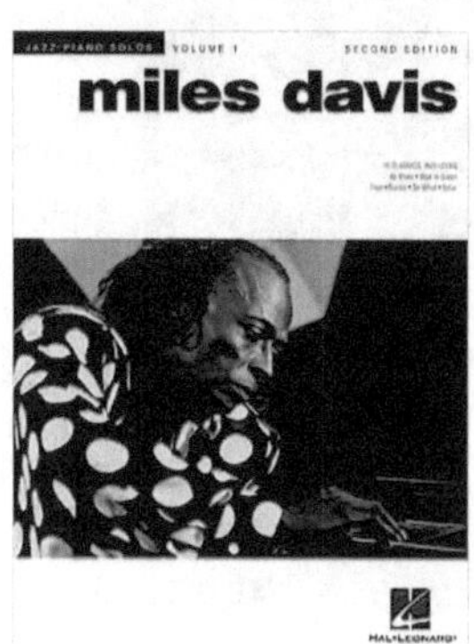

The Jazz Piano Solo series from Hal Leonard Corp includes not only Miles Davis and Smooth Jazz, but also piano performances such as Duke Ellington, Thelonious Monk, modern jazz quartet, Beatles, cool jazz, etc. There is. Arrangement is relatively simple, so it would be a good song collection to increase your repertoire.

『MESAR HAUS THEORY step』(Masahiko Satoh/Masar Haus) 2001

Textbook of "MUSIC COLLEGE MESAR HAUS". I have from I to VI (I don't know if there's anything after VI), but this textbook can learn a variety of things, such as note names, pitches, "chord progression", "harmony", and "voice arrangement". What I particularly like is that V is pretty detailed about modes. Most jazz textbooks only mention mode a little. Also, "scale" and "mode" have the same names, "Dorian" and "Mixoridian", which is confusing. In this regard, this book explains the nature of the mode fairly well, and I learned a lot.

『505 Great Piano Intros: Elegant Song Introductions Used by the Pros!』 (Kirk Miller/Alfred Publishing Company) 2001

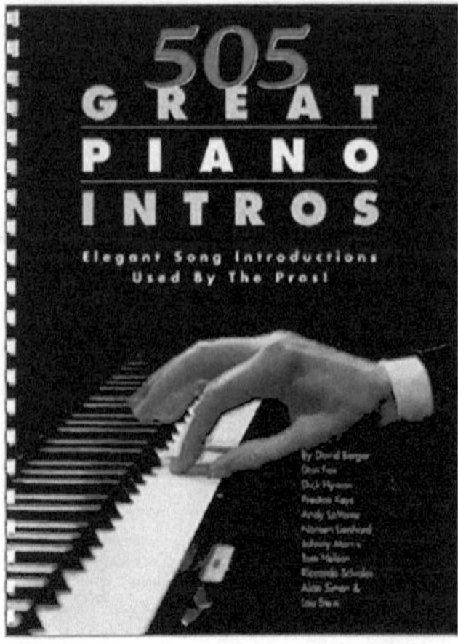

There are other intro textbooks, but this one is the most detailed.

Anyway, there are many intros that assume famous standards. They are categorized into Ballad, Medium Tempo, Up Tempo, LatinWaltz, Blues, Country, and Ellington styles. Authors include Dick Hyman, Preston Keys, Lou Stein, Dan Fox, Norreen Lienhard, Johnny Morris, Tom Nelson, Riccardo Scivales, Alan Simon, Andy LaVerne, David Berger. There is no theoretical explanation, but if you play it anyway, it will be sure that it will be helpful.

『Jazz Piano Solo Piano Concepts』 (Philipp Moehrke/ATN) 2002

To put it simply, this textbook is a study of the performance of famous jazz pianists. The author publishes songs based on the style of each pianist. With Errol Garner, Horace Silver, Georgie Shearing, Bud Powell, Keith Jarrett, McCoy Tyner, Eliane Elias and others, it's strange to see why Eliane is here. One such textbook is John Megan's etude, but this one is practical because each one is a song. Speaking of course, McCoy Tyner wanted the author to write a little more detail on how to play the right hand pentatonic.

I also wanted the author to include Keith Jarrett's country-style songs and Chick Korea's songs.

It comes with a CD so it will be very helpful.

『Jazz Piano Trio For Beginner』（Yukihiro Miyamae/Ritto Music）2002

Theoretically, it only explains the voicing of the left hand and the scale to be used, and as the author wrote, it is a teaching material of "Practice makes perfect". I think that training a classical piano often involves practicing alone for a long time and doing little ensemble, but in the case of jazz, it is better to play in a trio as in this book from the beginning. The songs are "Bags Groove", "Mornin", "Autum leaves", "Summer Time", "Take the A train", "Someday Prince", "The girl From Ipanema's daughter","My Funny Valentine" ", " Dolphin Dance ", " BalsaNova "and so on. The beginning "Bags and Grooves" can be played with only 6 notes.

However, the relationship between the book and the appendix CD is difficult to understand. Contrary to normal teaching materials, there are up to 10 tracks of bass and drum karaoke at first.And 11 to 20 are example performances including ad-lib. Does it mean to play first because everything is fine?

In addition, since 20 songs with only the theme that are not included in the CD are posted in front of the sample performance page, it is difficult to know which song is included in the CD.

『Performance Ability Exercise: Keyboard』（Dave Limina/ Rittor Music）2002

"This book was written by an author, an assistant professor at the Berklee College of Music, who offered a selection of menus that were effective in cultivating basic skills from piano exercises used in class, and that were musically attractive. There is a "training book", but the content is like a comping material. There are many examples of rock and blues, but for jazz pianists who want to play progressively, funk techniques that explain how to play such as Harvey Hancock, Stevie Wonder, Richard Tee are very helpful.

『The Chord Wheel: The Ultimate Tool for All Musicians』（Jim Fleser Hal/ Leonard Corp） 2002

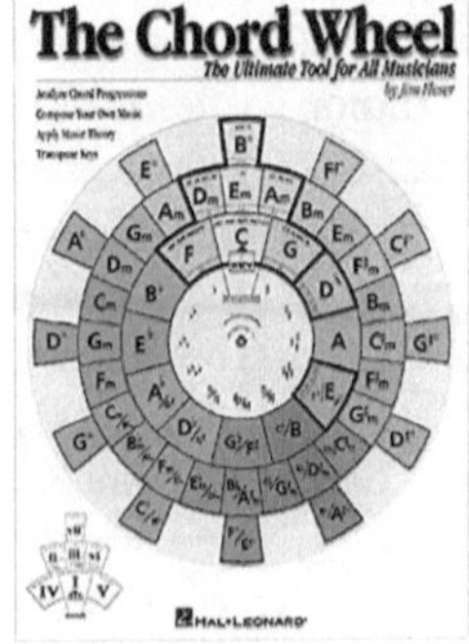

To explain th fifths e related key, it is easy to understand that it has a circle of fourths or fifths
This book is also a teaching material for such a method. However, it is movable with a panel wheel rather than a book. The usage is centered on your favorite key. For example, if Key is C, frequently used chords such as tonics, subdominants, dominants, substitute chords, etc. are displayed in a thick frame. Looking at these methods, I think that modern rationalism and functionalism are good.

『A Classical Approach to Jazz Piano Impovisation』(Dominic Alldis / Hal Leonard) 2003

Part 1 of Chapter 1 begins with the improvisation of Pentatonic. Pentatonic is often used in modal improvisation, so it can be said that it is learning for advanced users, but at the same time the master-slave relationship between sounds is not so defined, so even the first learner can freely improvise is there. In this sense, this book has a reasonable structure. Next to Pentatonic is a performance style in blues and be-bop. And again, Pentatonic, this time the advanced style of Pentatonic such as McCoy Tyner, left hand voicing, walking baseline practice, and a textbook that is very easy to learn for beginners.

『Jazz Piano Scales & Modes』(Misha Stefanuk /Mel Bay Publication) 2003

The textbook is about 100 pages, but mainly explains the available note scale for the code. For example, Cm7 (b5) describes available scales such as Locrian, Diminished-Whole-tone, Diminished-Whole-tone, Diminished-Half-Whole, Japanese4-Mode, and Bluse. He mentions Mode and other scales not mentioned in ordinary jazz theory books. However, as for specific usage examples, only a few examples of ad libs of Bluse and Bebop are posted, so I feel unsatisfactory.

『Just joking! Jazz piano』(Osamu Saito/ Rittor Music) 2003

To put it simply, a book on "fake" and "reharmonization" to play jazzy. There is not much explanation about adlib. Beethoven's "Song of Joy", "Aria on the G line", "One flower only in the world", "Let's walk up", etc. is there. Lastly, the theme of "Lupin III" is a song by jazz pianist Yuji Ohno, which is arranged in a cool way. A good textbook for first-time learners.

『Arranging for Large Jazz Ensemble』
(Ken Pullig and Dick Lowell / Berklee Press; Pap/Com edition) 2003

In the Big Band Arrangement textbook, "Inside the Score" based on the music actually played was a reputable textbook, but this book provides various techniques and analysis that are more detailed than that. The whole consists of 14 chapters. Chapter 1 explains the range, basic chords, scale, and harmonization of each instrument. The second chapter is Unison and Octave. Chapters 3 and 4 describe various harmonization styles including Fl, Sax, Tp, and Tb. Chapter 5 is the writing style of the fourth pitch. Chapter 6 is upper structure writing, and Chapter 7 is cluster writing. Chapter 8 is line style and Chapter 9 is mute style. Chapter 10 is sled writing. And the contents after Chapter 11 are examples of music. In particular, it will be very useful for studying the harmonization of how to stack each instrument.

『Hal LEONARD KEYBOARD STYLE SERIES・BEBOP JAZZ PIANO』
(JOHN VALERIO/Hal Leonard Corp)2003
『The same Title / POST−BOP JAZZ PIANO』(JOHN VALERIO/Hal
Leonard Corp)2005
『The same Title / Smooth jazz』(Mark Harrison/Hal Leonard Corp)
2005

This "Hal LEONARD KEYBOARD STYLE SERIES" series has many textbooks such as "Contemporary Jazz piano" and "Latin Jazz Piano" besides these three books. A good book that is affordable and practical in content. In brief, "BEBOP JAZZ PIANO" is written about the harmony and chord progression, ad-lib and comping used in Bebop in the first half, and the styles of Bud Powell and Thelonious Monk in the second half. For Bud Powell, there may be other textbooks, but for Thelonious Monk, it captures Monk's irony expression well. Recommended textbook for jazz piano beginners.

"POST-BOP JAZZ PIANO" describes how to play Bill Evans, Herbie Hancock, McCoy Tyner, Chick Korea, and Keith Jarrett. With an example performance by CD, it will be very helpful for those who want to play progressively. Among them, Bill Evans' harmony and Herbie Hancock's ad lib line are well expressed. For McCoy Tyner, I think the comping example is very good, but the right-hand pentatonic seems too simple.

As for Chick Korea, the outphrase of "Now Heatings Now He Sobbs" is posted from the beginning, and the unique rhythm of Latin style is also expressed well. Keith Jarrett well expresses the characteristics of harmony, but I also wanted him to take up a country-style performance.

You can think of "Smooth jazz piano" as a fusion. The harmony of Smooth jazz is not that complicated and the improvisation part is not long. However, for those who play only 4-beat jazz, it may seem that Smooth jazz's 8-beat and 16-beat performances are especially difficult to get rhythm. The model CD performance in this book is composed of two tracks. First, the piano, drum, and bass are played at slow speed, and then the piano, drum, bass, and synth are played at full speed. Because. If you practice along this, you will get a sense of Smooth jazz. By the way, there is "Contemporary Jazz piano" in the series・but the content is similar to "Smooth jazz piano". I will add that it is never a free jazz piano performance such as Cecil Taylor.

『HERBIE HANCOCK JAZZ PIANO』(HERBIE HANCOCK /Doremi Music Publishing) 2004

Speaking of Herbie Hancock, "Watermelon Man" was a hit in the 1960s, and he was active in the Miles Davis group. In the 1970s, "Headhunters", which introduced electric pianos and synthesizers, became a huge hit. "On the other hand, He doesn't forget the acoustic music in the VSOP Quintet, and" Future Shock "in the 1980s boldly introduced hip hop. He also became a leader in club music by DJ Scratch. This collection of songs reflects such various aspects of Hancock. Among them, "Four", "New York Minute" has 4 beats, "Watermelon man", "Maiden Vayage", "Cantaloupe Island" has 8 beats, "Sonrisa" and "The Essence" have 16 beats. This is a great teaching material for pianists who want to perform progressively but with a high degree of performance.

『Jazz Theory Work shop:Beginner,Intermediate & Advanced Edition』(Disen Koyama / Musashino Music School) 2004、2005

This book is a textbook used at Musashino Conservatory of Music.

Beginner's Chapter contains basic knowledge of overtones, equal temperament, intervals, scales, and chords before learning jazz in Chapters 1 and 2.

Chapters 3 and 4 describe chord functions and chord progression in general. Chapter 5 describes key relationships such as parallel, relative, and dominant key, and transposition. Chapters 6 and 7 describe the relationship between AvailableNote Scale and Tension.

It describes in detail how the melodies and phrases are made. Chapter 8 describes other knowledge about Cliche, Pedal point, Good Sound conditions and Diminishied Chord. Chapter 9 is the analysis of "Misty".

Chapter 1 of the middle and advanced editions provides detailed examples of various voices, such as the Chromatic Approach, the Altered Dominant Approach, and Reharmonization, and especially Contrary motion.

The second movement is a very detailed compilation of the Upper Structure Triad. Chapters 3 and 4 explain Mode, explain how Mode has been considered in the history of Western music, and deal with the techniques of Mode in Jazz. Chapter 5 describes the Combination of Diminished, and Chapter 6 describes bi-tonal, poly-tonal, poly-turn, and twelve-tone techniques. Chapter 7 explains fraction codes. Not only jazz, but also a variety of popular music, and a good book for those learning classical and contemporary music.

『The World of EiKo Hiroike-Jazz Born from Quantum Thinking (Jazz Critical Books)』(Eiko Hiroike/Mastuzaka) 2004

The author is a physicist (quantum theory) and also plays jazz piano.Often, "quantum theory" is often cited together with "relativity theory" as a natural science that supports contemporary art, but how is "quantum theory" related to jazz? In quantum theory, it is not fixed whether the nature of light is waves or particles. Is that related to jazz ad-lib performance? Regarding the published Psychedelic Phonon Dance, the author Hiroike stated, "" Everything that can be described by a wave according to quantum mechanics, the energy of the frequency of the wave multiplied by the constant of the blank is the energy of the magnitude. It can be described by having particles. The sound is a honey wave of the air, so physicists call the corresponding particles Phono. This song shows how Phonon dances in the air. Phonon goes straight through the air until it hits something and reflects. A CD related to this book has been released.

『Jazz Piano Technical Method : Practice of Jazz』 (Hisae Nakajima/Doremi Music Publishing) 2004

In short, this book is a training book for jazz piano. It's like jazz piano Hanon. Daily training is important, so a book like this may be necessary, but from the beginning to P155, scale training and arpeggio training are the main focus. These exercises get tired, so you need patience. The chord patterns and idioms from P156 are "Root and 7th" and "Left hand closed voicing" on the left hand, B-Bop-style phrases on the right hand, and "Open voicing" on P187. Most of them are mechanical exercises on the whole, but it is a very good textbook for improving skills.

『Michel Camilo (Adlib Perfect Copy)』（Shiori Aoyama/Shinko Music）2004

Even if you can play four beat jazz, Latin jazz piano needs a unique rhythm. You should study enough in this book. Performance of Camilo anyway there is no gap, is characterized by play without endlessly from the beginning to the end. All songs are original by Camilo, especially the performance of "Thinking of You" and "Caribe" are powerful. I think it would be nice to have a style of Latin jazz playing just one standard song in this book. That would be helpful. Certainly his technique is outstanding, but the composition seems simple. So listening to a lot of songs can get tired. After listening to Camilo, some people will want to hear Thelonious Monk.

『How to do improvisation-Listen to a CD! Music therapy session , Recipe collection』（Makoto Nomura 、Yusuke Kataoka/Aozora Music inc）2004

It's a very interesting book. It seems to be a textbook for music therapy, but it is a simple recipe book for improvisation. For example, if it is "What is environmental music", step on the pedal, play the lowest "D", and play white keys that are higher than the treble clef. Play sounds of various heights and enjoy the sound (laughs). In the case of "just kidding jazz", play the example with the left hand (when it was seen, it was a 4th chord). The right hand turns with a white key and turns it with a finger (laughs that Tamori(Japanese co entertainer) did). In the meantime, let's be more comfortable with how to do the music. Anyway, if you look at the score while listening to the CD, you will laugh unintentionally. Improvisation, on the one hand, requires advanced technology and knowledge, but on the other hand it has the ambiguity that anyone can do it. Anyway, you may want to try this book.

『Exploring Jazz Piano1.2』 (Time Richsrds / Schott) 2005

Volume 1 is recommended for first-time learners. Based on the author's songs, many basic chords up to the 9th, especially arpeggis, and many simple ad-lib exercises have been published.

Volume 2 features 9th, 11th, and 13th chords, Fourth Chords, modal voicing, and songs based on the explanation of each chord and scale. It comes with a CD, but only the theme is recorded, and the ad lib is not included in the book. There are quite a lot of these in American textbooks. This is a difference from the Japanese textbook.

『High Class Jazz Piano : Standard Number For Advanced』 (Yoshihiko Naya / Shinko Music)

The author, Yoshihiko Naya, remembers receiving the Best Soloist Award at the first Japan Jazz Grand Prix. This book is for advanced users, but some songs are easy to play, so it's more than intermediate. "Take the a train" Both hands are easy to play mainly in single tone, it would be a great song to master jazz. In "Night And Day", the ad-lib of the right hand while keeping the rhythm of the left hand is good for improving the technique. "My One And Only Love", "Body And Soul", and "Stardust" are perfect for ballad practice, and may be helpful in reharmonization. The left hand is often the 10th, so if you can't reach it, you need to devise it. With CD.

『High Grade Session Jazz Piano Score』 (Eriko Akitya /Shinko Music) 2005

It can be said that it is appropriate for advanced textbooks. "The Day Of Wine And Roses", "Donna Lee" and "I Love You Porgy" are perfect for Bebop practice. In particular, "Donna Lee" is a somewhat difficult song whose theme itself looks like an ad-lib. If you play enough, you will gain strength. The second half features the new mainstream Wayne Shorter "Footprnts", Herbie Hancock "Cantaloupe", Chick Korea "Spain" and "La Fiesta". These are features of this book that are not found in other textbooks. These songs will be a great reference for those who want to play progressively, such as using modal interpretation and using poly chords.

『Jazz Inventions for Keyboard: 50 Etudes That Will Improve the Way You Play Jazz』(Bill Cunliffe/Alfred Publishing) 2005

From the title Inventions, it wasn't the case if I thought it was a jazz version of Bach, like Jack Luche does.It's kind of like Jazz Czerny. Consists of 50 etudes. The main contents are basic chords, scales, practice of BeBop phrases, etc. No26's Five-VoiceChorale, Susp. Harmony, No27's "Polytonal Arpeggios", No47's "Line with Major Triad Pairs", etc. will be helpful for progressive performance.Such a training book gets tired while playing, but it will be useful because there are various variations and ideas.

『ContemporaryJazzPianoVol.3 Jazz Phrase Bilingual Edition』（Yasutoshi Inamori/Chyuou Art）2006

A phrase dictionary that lists all kinds of jazz phrases. And since it can be played in a variety of tones, the use of this book will broaden the scope as a pianist. If you want to play the first half Diatonic phrase or Altered dominant 7th scale for bebop-based ad-lib phrases, or the second half Perfect 4th Interval phrase or Pentatonic if you want to play progressive ad-lib phrases. However, the posting of Voicing on the left is barely mentioned, with only a small touch at the beginning. If posted, it would be a considerable number of pages, and the left hand wouldn't change as much as the right hand phrase, so it's a little disappointing for the player to think for himself.

『Fujii Eiichi Presents : Jazz piano Adlib Vol.1〜3』(Eiichi Fujii/YMM) 2006

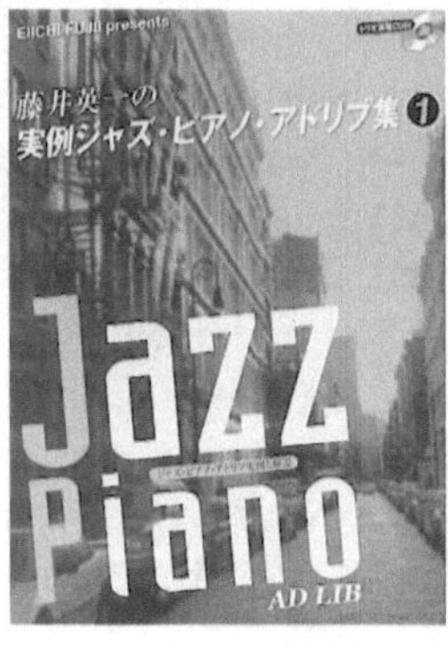

I would like to say that it is a resale book of "Jazz Piano Ad-lib Textbook 1.2.3" published in the early 80's and an ad-lib textbook of famous standard songs, but none of the themes are listed. You may not have wanted to pay the royalty fee. "~ Type" such as "TakeThe" A "depends on the chord progression of Train-type" or "Depends on the chord progression of Autumn Leaves - type". Even if there is no theme, it is good that the ad lib part is posted abundantly, but in American textbooks the opposite is only the theme, and the ad lib part is only code. In the age of "Jazz Piano Ad-lib Textbook", a cassette is included, and this book includes a CD. If you practice while listening to the sound source, you will gain strength, but when you play it, you will not get tired of coming out the same ad lib phrase many times.

『Eiichi Fujii Presents : Mozart In Jazz 』 (Eiichi Fujii / YMM) 2006

There have been many attempts to play classical music in jazz, such as Jacques Lucé and Eugen Cicero. This book is a textbook that plays the famous Mozart songs in a jazz arrangement. Published songs include "Piano Sonata No.8, No.11, No.15", "Aine Kleine Nacht Musik", "Symphony No.40, 41", "Piano Concerto No.20, No.23", etc. Although it is advanced, the arrangement is generally simple. The left hand is "Root and 7th", and the right hand is often single tone. These textbooks are also good for a change. Eiichi Fujii also has "Tchaikovsky in Jazz", "Japan in Jazz" and "Bach in Jazz".

『Changes Over Time The Evolution Of Jazz Arrangement
〈Fred Sturm、Japanese Translation By Atsuhito Aikawa/ ATN〉2006

Based on 4 songs, Jelly Roll Morton's "King Porter Stomp" Don Redman's "Chant of the Weed" Gerald Marks and Seymour Simon's "All of Me" and Billy Strayhorn's "Take The 'A' Train" 35 arrangements were made by Jazz Alangers including Don Redman, Fletcher Henderson, Benny Carter, Duke Ellington, Billy Strayhorn, Gil Evans, Thad Jones, Bill Holman, Bob Brookmeyer, and Clare Fischer. Characteristic rhythms, melodies, harmonization, orchestration, etc. are picked up and explained. This book provides a glimpse of the historical and technical changes in music, showing how the same music differs from period to period and from musician to musician. This book is not written by a first learner, but it is a perfect textbook for those who want to try out big band ranges.

『GREAT JAZZ PIANO SOLO1.2』（Wise Publications） 2006、2007

Songs published in Vol.1

『Ain't Misbehavin' (Fats Waller)』、『Between The Devil And The Deep Blue Sea (Diana Krall)』、『Blue Monk (Thelonious Monk)』、『Blue Rondo A La Turk (Dave Brubeck)』 『Bouncing With Bud (Bud Powell)』、『Cantaloupe Island (Herbie Hancock)』、『Chelsea Bridge (Duke Ellington)』、『I Wish I Knew How It Would Feel To Be Free (Billy Taylor)』 『Innocence (Keith Jarrett)』、『King Porter Stomp (Jelly Roll Morton)』、『Love Is Just Around The Corner (Earl Hines)』、『Moonglow (Art Tatum)』、『My Baby Just Cares For Me (Nina Simone)』、『Song For My Father (Horace Silver)』、『Splanky (Count Basie)』、『Take Five (Dave Brubeck)』、『The Girl From Ipanema (Oscar Peterson)』、『Two Lonely People (Bill Evans)』、『Waltz For Debbie (Bill Evans)』、『Well You Needn't (It's Over Now) (Thelonious Monk)』

Songs published in Vol.2

『Don't Know Why (Norah Jones)』、『Lullaby Of Birdland (George Shearing)』、『Take The 'A' Train (Duke Ellington)』、『Maple Leaf Rag (Scott Joplin,)、『Caravan (Duke Ellington,)、(Tizol, Juan)、(Irving Mills)』、『Misty (Erroll Garner)』、『Honeysuckle Rose (Waller, Fats)、『Georgia On My Mind (Ray Charles)』『Ruby My Dear (Thelonious Monk,)』、『Peri's Scope (Bill Evans)』、『Do Nothing Till You Hear From Me (Duke Ellington, Bob Russell)』、『Monk's Mood (Thelonious Monk)』

『In Your Own Sweet Way (Dave Brubeck)』、『Get Your Way (Jamie Cullum)』

『Blues On The Corner (McCoy Tyner,)』、『Desafinado (Jobim Antonio Carlos)』

『Maiden Voyage (Herbie Hancock,)』、『Quiet Night Of Quiet Stars (Corcovado) Antonio Carlos Jobim,』、『Doing The Bird Cage Walk (Later...With Jools Holland) (Jools Holland)』 (Gilson Lavis,))、『Now He Sings, Now He Sobs (Chick Corea,)』、『Yesterdays (Dudley Moore,)』

Many of these Transcription songs are re-used in other books. I don't think Keith Jarrett's "Innocence" has been featured in other books, but it's invaluable because Keith's performance is well-characterized. I think Errol Garner's "Misty" is now often played on Eb, but this book is on Transcription, Ab from Garner's first recording. This performance is the simplest and most beautiful. Anyway, the luxurious lineup will be very helpful.

『Professional Jazz Piano』(Keiji Matsumoto/ Ymaha Music Media) 2007

This is an advanced course textbook. This one is more pop and novel compared to textbooks by Yoshihiko Naya and Eriko Akiya, also for advanced users. There are 11 standard songs and 3 original songs by Keiji Matsumoto. Up-tempo songs such as "Autumn Leaves" and "Stella by Starlight" are mechanical ad lib phrases because the right hand uses many chromatic phrases. The left hand is a style that slides the inner voice without a walking bassline. Re-harmonization of slow ballads such as "Alfie" and "Over The Rainbow" will be very helpful because they have a good taste. Each original song feels like country rock and the adlib sounds like Keith Jarrett. I personally like the melody of "Playback", but the transpositioned phrase is too stiff or unclear in which direction it evolves. That might sound more progressive though.

『 Contemporary Jazz PianoVol4：The Jazz Chords・Bilingual Edition 』(Yasutoshi Inamori/Chyuou Art) 2007

This book is a jazz code dictionary. Contains all the codes used in jazz. Chapter 1 explains the basic code, Chapter 2 describes left hand voicing. Chapter 3 describes voicing with two handed chords, polychords, and chords of quadruple chords, taking various songs as examples. In addition, since P122, a lot of code work of both hands is published in the code. After P223, an example of comping is shown. Even if it's a chord dictionary, if you're a beginner to jazz piano, this book is too complicated to use.

For those who can play jazz to some extent, it would be better to use this book to give them a wider range of performance or as an idea for re-harmonization.

『60 ways to improve your piano』(Shigehito Suzuki/Shinko) 2008

So to speak, a material about playing piano.
The contents are divided into "POPS", "JAZZ", and "CLASSC", but there are 60 patterns in all, so you can learn a lot. In particular, JAZZ's "Phrases that improve octave ad lib", "Phrases that improve melody rehabilitation", and "Phrases that improve free mode ad lib", which require advanced techniques, are clear and easy to understand. However, since each is about eight measures, it is not clear whether the piano will improve dramatically even if it gives hints on performance and composition. To improve, you'll need to play more transposed or use the patterns in this book for a variety of songs.

『Playing jazz piano』 (Bob Mintzer /Alfred Pub Co) 2008

Although it is a 43-page textbook, 22 exercises that make learners aware of the functions of Sound, Texture, Cause, Effect, and jazz code, etc., consist of various styles, tempos, and chord progressions. Exercise is not too tired because each is a short song. The techniques to be learned are clearly indicated as "The Blues Comp Chords"- "Rhythm Changes Right-Hand Solo", "Standard Right-Hand Solo", and "Standard Comp with BassLine".

『Excellnt Jazz Solo Piano (With CD)』(DodoToru/Rotto Music) 2008

it is a very good textbook. The performance of the first song, "Pictures at an Exhibition-Promenade", is not so jazzy, but is interpreted dignifiedly. "Days Of Wine And Rose" is very helpful for inner voice movements. The Latin piano playing style of "The Shadow of Your Smile" is interesting. Satie's "Gymnopedie No1" is likely to ruin the image of the song if carelessly ad-libd, but I think the arrangement of this book is very good because it is finished in a simple and colorful interpretation. Also, the rehabilitation of "As Time Goes By" is very helpful. It is a textbook that you can train while having fun. With CD.

『Contemporary Jazz Piano 1,2,3』（Nohiko Hojo/Chyou art ）
2008～2012

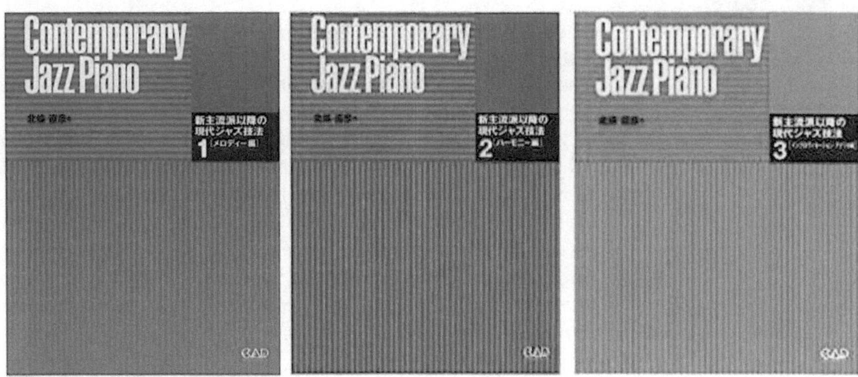

Naohiko Hokujo is a composer from Tokyo University of the Arts, and his classmate is composer Shinichiro Ikebe.

While active as a jazz pianist, he is also a composer of contemporary music.

This book consists of three volumes, but a textbook about jazz techniques after modal that Miles and Coltrane opened up. Speaking of pianists, it describes how to play McCoy Tyner, Herbie Hancock, Chick Korea, Keith Jarrett, and Richie Beirach.

Perhaps there aren't many other jazz piano textbooks written by Japanese people about these jazz, and this textbook has a more detailed analysis than Bill Dobbins' The Contemporary Jazz Pianist. Because it is made, it can be said that it is an epoch-making textbook.

Introducing each one, the first volume is "Melody", the pentatonic playing technique of Tic Korea, Ritchie Bailark, Coltrane ad lib as an example, chord progression from inside, outside, Triad, The discussion from Polychord, various developments of the Mode technique, Modal Change, Polymode, etc. are written.

Volume 2 is written with a focus on modal harmony. "Quartal", "Quintal", "Secondal", "Hybrid", "Colortone", etc. Each modal voicing, contry motion, constant structure, etc.

Volume 3 is reharmonisation of songs such as "I got rhythm", "But not for me" and "Summertime" by Hojo himself, and analyses songs of Richie Beirach, Herbie Hancock and Chick Korea.

『Berklee Jazz Piano』 (Ray Santisi/Berklee Pr Pubns)2009

Author Ray Santisi is a pianist who has long taught at Berklee College of Music. The content of this book is harmonization for chords and melodies. Introduction of tension. A series of articles, such as Walking Bass Line, Open Voicing, Upper Structure Triads, Approach note Harmonization, Pentatonic Scales and Chords. Modal Melody and Chords, have been published. There is no special content that is covered only in this book, and since it is a textbook of about 100 pages, the number of actual examples of each is small,Still, the explanation is clear and easy to understand. Only the latter half of Etudes' songs are played on the appendix CD, but it is very useful for learning Harmonization, especially the Parallel Approach.

『Bill Evans Perfect Piano Socre (With CD)』 Tomoyuki Hayashi Doremi Music Publishing)2010

If the father of a modern jazz piano is Bud Powell, the established person may be Bill Evans. The fact that Bill Evans Transcription appears at the beginning of John Megan's masterpiece "Modern Piano Style", which was introduced in this book, also demonstrates this. By the way, in Japan, Bill Evans seems to have the image of a pianist playing a romantic performance. But rather, his performance has a cold image. That may be due to his mental weakness, as opposed to the perfection of his playing, as he could not get along with drugs to the end. Evans's charm, however, may be the human shade and yang, or the light and shade. Bill Evans's Transcription has been published a lot, but I took this book up for complete transcription. It will be very useful for all Jass pian

『Super Practical! Jazz Piano School Learn from 20 Famous Jazz Pianist "Jazzy" how to play』 (Yukihiro Miyamae.Taku Yamamoto ,Hidesuke Kato, Ryuta Aniru, Shinichiro Imai/Ritto Music)2011

Thelonious Monk, Red Garland, Bud Powell, Oscar Peterson, Bill Evans, McCoy Tyner, Joe Sampling, Herbie Hancock, Chick Korea, Chucho Valdes, Kenny Barron, Sesame Camargo Mariano , Keith Jarrett, Michel Camilo, Kenny Kirkland, Brad Mehldau, and more. The Thelonious Monk's "whole tone scale", Red Garland's" block chords", and McCoy Tyner's "pentatonic" are familiar. But I don't think Kenny Barron, Sesame Camargo Mariano, and Kenny Kirkland's playing techniques are often featured in other textbooks.

『The reason why jazz piano can be played well and the reason for bad performance』(Hideaki Hori/Ritto Music) 2011

The whole is roughly divided into "Technique", "Chord / Work", "Rhythm", and "Session", which are further divided into "Symptoms", "Causes", and "Measures". For example, if the symptom is "I can't use Blue Note well," the cause is "1. I can't use the characteristic sound of Blue Note Scale. 2. It's a simple performance. As a countermeasure, "1. Know the characteristic sound and use it in a phrase. 2. Attack with heavy sounds. 3. Try to express the trivial blues of everyday life." Typical performances are introduced.

I think there are many places that can be helpful to learners as a whole. However, it is neither a training book nor a songbook, so I don't think this book alone will improve. As the title suggests, it is better to think of it as a reading material that understands why a jazz piano can be played well.

『Scale & Solo phrases for pianists BOOK (with CD)』(Akihiro Horikoshi/Ritto Music) 2011

In a nutshell, it can be said that it is a book that explains the scale used in jazz popular music, but in general, every page shows the scale on the left page, the voice on the left and the voice on both hands, and examples of phrases ing. It's neither a training book nor a songbook, so it might be a good way to use it lexicographically if you're stuck with an idea. Music is more abstract than everyday language but a kind of language. Therefore, I think that the four principles of language can be applied to music as it is. With that in mind, it seems good to think of scale as idioms and grammar needed to speak. The more you know, the richer your vocabulary will be and the more convincing you can play.

『 PENTATONICISM IN JAZZ : CREATIVE ASPECTS AND PRACTICE 』 (Masaya Yamaguchi/Doremi Music Publishing) 2011
『SYMMETRICAL SCALES FOR JAZZ IMPROVISATION』 (Masaya Yamaguchi/DoremiMusic Publishing) 2011

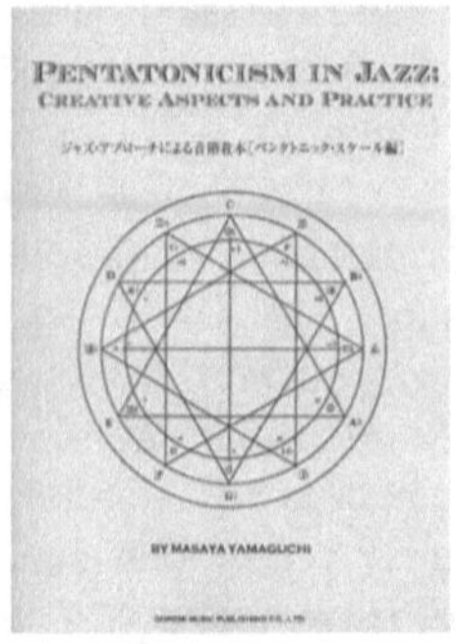

The upper left is "Pentatonic". As I mentioned in other textbooks, Pentatonic is not a major / minor scale. Since the master-slave relationship between the sounds is not clear, the player can freely ad-lib. Therefore, it is easy for beginners to play. On the other hand, it has the character that it is often used for advanced ad-lib, such as the mode playing method, such as the performance of Coltrane and McCoy Tyner, which tried to release from the complicated harmony.

This book describes the "66 pentatonic scale", which shows all the possibilities of pentatonic. In addition to the original pentatonic, you will learn "Diminished Pentatonic", "Altered 7th Pentatonic", and "2-5 sound pattern" depending on the interval.

The upper right is "Symmetrical Scale". WholeTone Scale, Diminished Scale, etc. are written by any jazz theory office as "Symmetrical Scale" (a scale that has a symmetrical structure that returns to its original state by repeating the transposition operation) invented by Messiaen. A scale is added, and using these scales, a pattern of a four- or three-tone sound group structure having pitches of 3 to 6 degrees that goes up and down is learned. It is also a feature of this book that explanations are provided not only with staff paper but also with a series of numbers.

Both textbooks will be helpful in performing progressive performances.

『Jazz Piano Method :Theory&Training』（Akimitsu Iwase/Saber inc）2012

Learn about various scale exercises, left hand voicing with tension, spread (including left hand Root and 7th, Root, and 3th), open voicing and drop 2, Upper Structure Triad, and chord work. It is good that you can practice with various keys. For example, Drop2 etc. which are published in 105p-117p are only one or two examples of other textbooks, but in this book you can practice with all keys. It is a very good book as a training book.

『Jazz Piano Advances : Jazz Standrd 40 Vol.1』（YMM）2012

Includes 40 songs, including "The Things You Are", "Lullaby Of Birdland", "Take The" A "Train", "A Night In Tunisia", "Satin Doll", and "Nica's Dream". "The Things You Are" and "Someone To Watch Over Me" are arrangements that are quite playable. "Blue Monk" also expresses the characteristics of the performance of Thelonious Monk. Even so, the appearance of playing such a jazz music collection is often posted on video sites, but despite playing complex arrangements well, I feel that playing is unnatural. Because your performance is not improvised, it is not your own original performance. Therefore, those who want to play jazz piano in earnest should refer to such a collection of songs.

『Adlib　Method for Jazz Piano1.2』(Shigeru Kawashima/ Chyuo Art Piblishing）2013

A textbook to practice with 12 keys. As mentioned in the textbook of Sadayasu Fujii introduced earlier, many jazz pieces are flat type, such as C, F, Bb, and Eb in major and Am, Dm, Gm, Cm in minor. However, considering that modulations and substitute chords appear everywhere, practicing with 12 keys expands the skills and musicality of the pinist. Compared to Sadayasu Fujii's textbook, which does not include any left-hand texts, this book is easier to practice because the left-hand code is written. It is a recommended textbook for daily training.

『Big Band Jazz Arrangement』(Yu Ktagawa/kyutaryumu）2013

There were many big bands in Japan such as Blue Coats, Tokyo Union and New Hard. Also Once upon a time, The big band was playing accompaniment to the popular singer. That means learning to arrange a big band means learning to arrange popular music. Now that professional big bands are almost gone, student big band activity seems to be thriving. This book details the approach of harmonization (resolution), such as the distinction between tension and approach notes, while increasing the number of section parts. However, this book has no exercise at all, so it may not be possible for anyone who wants to arrange a big band to get an idea of where to start. I wanted an exercise for each theme or for each chapter, and I wanted it to be in a step-by-step configuration so that if I understood this technique, I could make it this far.

『The Jazz Harmony Book』(David Berkman/Sher Music Co) 2013

This book is a harmonization textbook on how to add effective harmony to melodies. Starting with the basic dominant motion chord progression, it details the re-harmonization of "Passing Diminished", "Modal Interchang", "Tritone Substitute", "Diminishied Chord". Each is about 4 bars, but examples of harmonization of famous songs such as "Take the A train", "The girl from ipanema", "Body and Soul", "Silent Night" and "Night and Day" are shown. However, "These Foolish Things" and "In a Sentimental Mood" are all harmonized. It has two CDs so you can learn effectively.

『An Approach to Comping: The Essentials』(Jeb Patton /Sher Music) 2013
『An Approach to Comping Vo.2: Advanced Concepts &   Technique 』(Jeb Patton /Sher Music) 2016

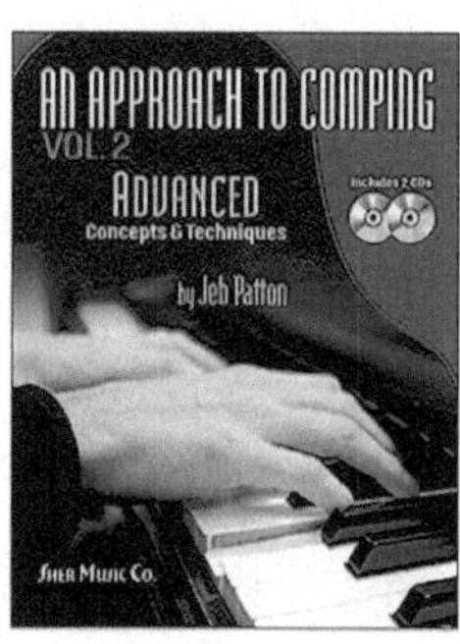

This book is a comping (backing) textbook. I think comping practice is very important for jazz pianists. Playing the piano alone is good, but sessions with other performers are fun. Also, when the pianist is comping, you will be supporting other performers, so it will promote otherness within you and grow your performance. I was able to play "Autum leaves" and "Satin dolls", and this time when I had a session with saxophone, guitar, and piano trio, it was difficult to find out how to camping. Also, the guitar and piano chords overlapped during the performance, which was a problem. There are other textbooks dedicated to comping, but this book is especially recommended.The first half of the first volume (left) focuses on playing chords in triplet rhythm. By doing so, you can learn the jazz rhythm and "ride" and connect it to comping. Volume 2 (right) shows many examples of comping by famous players (Bill Evans, McCoy Tyner, Herbie Hancock, etc.). In addition, the music included in the attached CD has a very good sound quality, and it contains saxophone and trumpet performances, so it has a sense of presence and is wonderful.

『100 JAZZ LESSONS KEYBOARD LESSON』(Brent Edstrom, Peter Deneff / Hal Leonard Corp)2014

It is a very interesting textbook.

Since it is about 100 LESSON, there are 100 different ways of playing about Scales, modes, jazz styles, improvement methods, harmonic voicings, etc. "Altered Dominant Scale", "Arpeggiating" Through the hanges "," Funky Comping "," Drop-2 Voicing "," Scale-Tone Voicing "," Bebop Blues "," Power Voicing "," Extended Harmony "," Using " Diminished Scales "," Comping Concepts "," Pentatonic to Mixolydian ", etc. However, they are all touching. Although the content of each lesson is not detailed, it will be very good for basic practice.

『I teach jazz piano practice (With CD)』(Yoshifumi Noro/ Doremi Music Publishing)2014

From the beginning until 120P, I practice scales and arpeggios just like Hanon. I don't think that such practice is necessary for those who can play the piano to some extent learning jazz piano.

"Tension chord" after 120p, "Alter do tension", "Back chord", "Combination of diminished scale", "Minor tension cord and scale", "Blue note ad lib", etc. Each practice will also play with 12 keys, so you will gain strength.

However, exercise is monotonous as a whole, so if you do not devise a sharpness such as playing songs while practicing such, you will get tired and will not last long.

『Jazz theory』 (Dariusz Terefenko /Routledge) 2014

It is a large book with 465 pages, but it is not an esoteric book but the contents are very easy to understand. In particular, Bebop's description uses "Confirmation" and "Moose The Mooche" as examples, but it explains in detail how the basics of jazz ad-lib are made. The other chapter, "Pentatonics And Hexatonics", explains the relationship between scale and chord in a clear way. The "Post Tonal Jazz" chapter contains a lot of cluster-like harmony that hits the Semitone, so it will be helpful to understand progressive jazz. With DVD (only sound source).

『Modal Diatonicism (Harmonic and Melodic Music Theory and Method for the 21st Century)』(Adrian Allen/Createspace Independent Pub) 2014

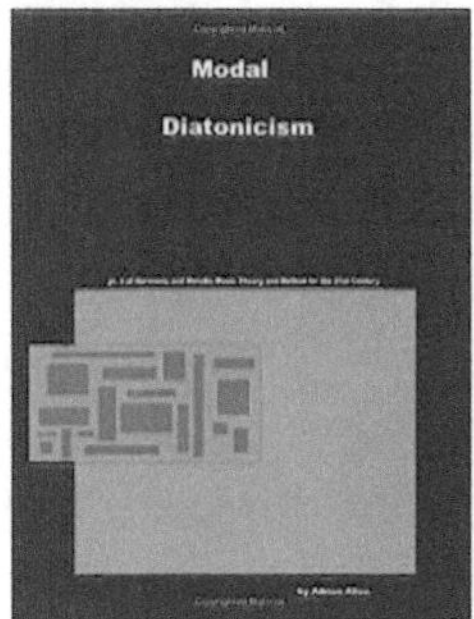

Although this book is not particularly a jazz textbook, it focuses on the mode used in jazz (church mode).

Various patterns are described, such as the case where the fundamental is the same and the mode is converted, and the case where the mode is the same and the fundamental is converted. However, Voicing is not the fourth interval build often used in the mode, but the triad. In this case, if a functional code is easily added to the mode, the characteristics of the mode may be lost, but the details are unknown because there is only one music example. Most of them are only listed using the scale used in steps. The names often used for modes such as durian and mixolidian are also misunderstood because they are also used for the available note scale derived from chord progression. However, this book is not such an example.

『Hal Leonard Jazz Piano Method : The Plaver's Guide to Authentic Stylings』(Mark Davis/ Hal Leonard Corp) 2015

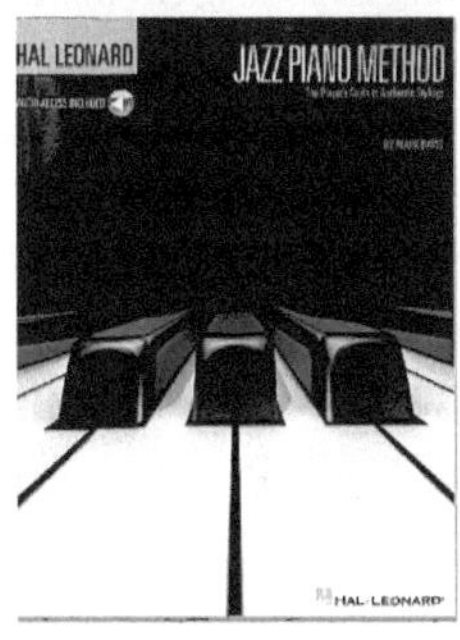

It starts with basic scales, chords, and voicing, but especially chapters 5 through 7 explain in detail how to do ad lib. You will especially learn how to use approach notes.

Although there is no explanation of progressive theory such as Upper Structure or Poly Chord, it can be said that it is the best textbook for new learners of Jazz piano, mainly playing Bebop.

All of the published music sources can be downloaded from the web.

『Practice! Ultimate Jazz TheoryTo Learn in Earnest』 (Yasuto Hikosaka/Jiyu Gendaisya）2015

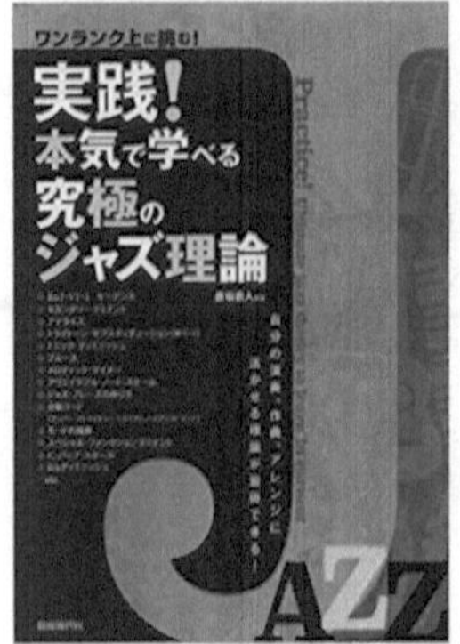

The textbook is polite and easy to understand. In particular, the Ave Iravel note scales are easy to understand, so it will be useful to organize and memorize each scale. Also, the fact that Tonic Diminish is written over seven pages is a feature not described in other textbooks.

Harmonization isn't written much in detail, but it may be to refer to the author's Popular Harmonics.

It is a recommended textbook for beginners.

『Jazz piano Textbook Vol.1 For Basic』、『The same Title Vol.2 For Advenced』（Yoshifumi Noro/Doremi Music Publihsing）2016

"Basic" at the top left is the practice of chords and scales necessary for jazz piano.It's written with 12 keys, so I think it's very good for basic exercises, but it's always tedious to do these kinds of exercises every day. In order to keep the learners from getting bored, I think it is necessary to add tunes everywhere to make them sharp.

The upper right is for people who can play the jas piano to some extent. The beginning is how to make an ad-lib with Dominant Tomotion. Ad lib with tension notes, ad lib with blue notes, ad lib with modes. Performance with various rhythm patterns from page 52. "Drop 2", "4th interval build", "Upper Structure Triad" etc. from page 72 have theoretical explanations, but no actual examples have been shown. The introduction and ending from page 81 will be quite helpful. Overall a reasonable textbook.

『The Principles of Music』(Hideaki Kondo/ Artes Piblishing)2016

A large book that covers 576 pages.
Considering that "music cannot be made from music", it would be appropriate to discuss music from all angles as in this book. This is because human beings are not only physical but also self-conscious, including unconscious. Therefore, it is necessary to always consider not only the observer's standpoint but also how the internal change of the self is connected to the world. About 40 pages of jazzare written, but there are characteristic and important points. Please read this book. Rather than music, I would recommend it to all sound professionals and learners.

『100 Ultimate Soul, Funk and R&B Grooves for Piano/Keyboards 』 (Andrew D. Gordon/A.D.G. Productions) 2016

There are many jazz piano textbooks written by Japanese, but they are rarely found in R & B and Funk textbooks. If you think that if you can play Jazz, you can easily play Funk and so on, that's a mistake. Even if you can play 4-beat jazz, it doesn't always mean you can play Funk's piano right away. Sure, playing a jazz piano is all you need for chord work, but it's difficult to play Funk's 16 beats in In tempo with alternating rhythms with your left and right hands.

I guess Funk's textbook was originally written by author D. Gordon, "60 Of The Funkiest Keyboard Riffs Known To Mankind" (1995). The book introduces 60 patterns (all about 9 bars), but here are 100 patterns including James Brown, Herbie Hancock, The Crusaders, Average White Band, Marvin Gaye, Miles Davis, Stevie Wonder, etc. Have been. However, each is about 4 bars. Voising is not difficult even if you say that it is the most difficult to grasp the rhythm, so if you get used to rhythm patterns, you can play basic chords and sometimes use a chromatic approach without depending on music. Will be.

『Essential Elements for Jazz Ensemble』(MikeSteinel, Japanese Translation By KzuhiroTkeda /ATN)2018

This is a very good book.
However, there is little description of the available note scale used for ad lib, and there is no description about harmonization, block chode etc. However, it is a textbook that tries to play anything and swing, that is, to learn jazz . For a jazz piano beginner, this textbook would be very good. Overall, the blues performance is described in detail. For beginners, using blue notes makes ad-lib easier. This book also explains how to create be-bop phrases, so if you practice over and over, you will be able to play jazzy ad-libs.

『Nogizaka46 Enjoying Piano Solo Jazz Arrangement』 (Presto/YMM)2019

You can't be foolish just because it's a jazz arrangement of an idol song.There is only advanced level, and it is more difficult than the basic and intermediate level of "Jazz Standard Masterpieces".
I mentioned earlier that it was difficult to play a jazz arrangement song collection of "Tatsuro Yamashita" and "Mariya Takeuchi", but this is the same. It is rich in varieties such as 4 beat swing, ballad, jazz waltz, bossa nova, etc.
I think the arrangement is well done, but this way, Nogizaka 46 seems to be a good jazz song.
But would a jazz piano learner really buy an idol songbook (make it a repertoire)?

『Jazz Pano Japan』 (Jacob Koller/ Jacob Koller international School) 2019

Author Jacob Koller is a jazz pianist living in Japan from Phoenix, USA. His performances have a high level of classical as well as jazz.
This book is a collection of arrangements featuring Japanese anime theme songs, pops, and nursery rhymes. There are 17 songs, including "The mmerry-go-round of life", "Sakura Sakura", "Paprika", "Ellie My Love", "Akatonbo", "Sora Ni Hoshi Ga Aru You Ni" and "Galaxy Express 999".
There are a variety of playing styles such as 4 beat jazz, ballads and funk, but all are difficult to play. If you can play them well, it is cool. So it's worth the challenge.

I picked up the particularly recommended ones from the Jazz piano textbooks introduced in this book. (However, music collection and Transcription (copy collection) are excluded.) For details, please see the text.

Beginner

* 『Hal Leonard Jazz Piano Method: The Player's Guide to Authentic Stylings』 (Mark Davis)
* 『Jazz Piano Concepts & Techniques』(John Valerio)
* 『Hal LEONARD KEYBOARD STYLE SERIES・BEBOP JAZZ PIANO』 (JOHN VALERIO)
* 『A Classical Approach to Jazz Piano Impovisation』 (Dominic Alldis)
* 『Jazz piano Adlib Master』 (Atsuo Kotani/ Rittor Music)
* 『Adlib Method for Jazz Piano1.2』(Shigeru Kawashima)
* 『Easy Jazz Piano 』(Naoki Nishi)
* 『With CD EiicHi Fujii Jazz Piano Training』(Eiichi Fujii)

More than Intermediate

* 『The Jazz Piano』 (Mark Levine)
* 『ComtemporaryJazz PianoVol.1,2』(Tasutoshi Inamori,Naohiko Hojo)
* 『The Contemporary Keyboardist』(John Novello)
* 『Jazz Piano Solo Piano Concepts』(Philipp Moehrke)

Advanced

* 『The Contemporary Jazz Pianist1〜4』(Bill Dobbins)
* 『Contemporary Jazz Piano1〜3』(Nohiko Hojo)

Composition, Arrangement&Theory

* 『MESAR HAUS THEORY step』(Masahiko Sato)
* 『Practical Seminar Of Jazz-Vol.Theory Edition』』(Sadayasu Fujii)
* 『Contemporary Keybord Chord Work』(Tomoyuki Hayashi/Rittor Music)
* 『Practical Popular Music Arrangment』(Genichi Kawakami /Yamaha Music Shinkoukai)
* 『Arranging Project For Today's Music』』(Eiji Kitahara)
* 『Arranging Comcepts 』(Dick Grove)
* 『The Contemporary Arranger』(Don Sebesky)
* 『Modal Jazz Composition & Harmony Vol. 1、2』(Ron Miller)
* 『Jazz & PopTheory Serie : Arrangement (With CD)』(Takayuki Hirano/YMM)

3. About Web Learning

The Roots music school mentioned earlier had used the Web to conduct jazz piano distance learning. I don't seem to do it now, but when I saw it, I thought that the learning environment had finally come this far, but that is now common. Berklee College of Music can also earn degrees through web courses, and the internet has changed the learning environment considerably. In recent years, jazz popular courses have been launched at many music colleges in Japan, and as in the past, studying classics at the music college in the daytime and studying at the jazz popular music school in the evening, the double school is going away. Due to the diversification of the learning environment and the declining birth rate, many jazz schools such as Musashino music school, Lovely Music School and Pan Music School have been closed down. It can be said that competition for survival is fierce.
Under such circumstances, I would like to introduce about two new learning styles.

* Udemy (https://www.udemy.com)

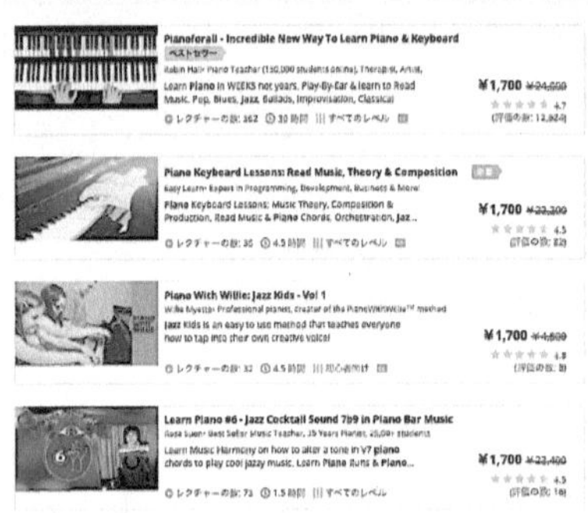

There are now many web-based learning sites, but I would like to introduce Udemy in that it is available to everyone.

To date, Udemy has 55,000 courses in marketing, business skills, foreign languages and web design. Music includes composition, jazz, classical piano, guitar, voice training, theory, and DTM. Among them, jazz piano had about 300 courses. (See left figure)

One lesson in one course is easy to take, from 5 to 15 minutes. In college, one class takes 90 minutes, but today's students may not be able to concentrate on 90 minutes. If such a learning site is made, the only difference from a university is whether a degree can be earned or not? When I took the jazz piano course as a trial, some of them were linked to see the jazz piano Transcription on youtube, and some were lectured using only other sites. And those who are giving lectures here are not teachers but instructors. What is the difference between a teacher and an instructor? In my opinion, Teachers are attracted to students by combining such human charm with content, such as their own experiences, failures, boasting stories, and jokes. But the instructor teaches only the points that seem to stand up soon. Therefore, popular courses will have a high income, but courses without attendees may be discontinued.

＊Scribd（https://ja.scribd.com）

The site, Scribd, is an open publishing platform that has 60 million books and documents on the Web to date. There are a lot of jazz textbooks as well, but there are free and paid courses, and even paid courses cost around 1,000 yen per month, and you can download as many books as PDF.
If you look at it, you can download a lot of jazz textbooks in a short time.

If people share files with each other, a sharing society that does not cost as a whole is not necessarily bad.
Because in Japan, 7 million tons of still-edible food are discarded each year.
The same applies to books.
Publisher publish a large number of books one after another in the way that they get money from one person to cover a debt to another person and discard those books.
In that sense, what we need to do now is to bring the necessary information to the people who need it, and to reform our self-consciousness without excessive possession.

4. About learning methods

It may already be obvious, but I would like to summarize jazz textbook learning.

* Perfect one book

It is effective not only for jazz textbooks but also for various qualification examinations, but when you challenge an unknown field, you must first complete one textbook.

Until you finish one book, don't touch other textbooks. To that end, there should be as thin a book as possible rather than a thick textbook. It is better to complete one book and memorize what is written on which page. Because jazz is improvised, you might think it would be meaningless to memorize it completely, but in the first stage you need to memorize it. Repeated practice is essential for memorization. Music is also a kind of language, although it is more abstract than everyday language. Therefore, by repeating, new neurons that connect cells are formed, and the link system between words and words and sounds and sounds naturally develops. In addition, if you complete one book, you will be confident and improve the learning efficiency when you proceed to the second and third books.

*Importance of copying

Dictation (simultaneous "writing" and "listening") and reading aloud (simultaneous "speaking" and "reading") are two powerful methods of language acquisition.

If you compare it to music, the former will be listening and the latter will be singing.

 In the past, when there were no textbooks, copying sound from records was the only learning method. I think that is still a very effective method. Even in the era when there are many Transcriptions today, we recommend that you copy from the player's sound source yourself.

* Practice in 12 keys

Jazz standard music is C, F, Bb, Eb for major keys, Am for minor keys, Dm, Gm, Cm are made with an overwhelmingly flat key. Therefore, the text is often written in a flat key. However, even the key of the C major often changes the key by the substitute chord and transposition. Therefore it is ideal to be able to play any key. Then you will improve as a player. For example, if you were able to play jazz brilliantly with only your key, and someone asked you to accompany a pop song, and that song was a # series song, if you could play well, You will be trusted.

* How to learn continuously

How you can play well is the same as how you can continue. The answer is clear. Either you want to integrate what you want to master into your everyday life or use it at work. For example, Japanese people who are good at English are almost always those who have set themselves up in an environment where they cannot live without English, or have used them at work.

Most people have forgotten what you learned in high school, such as "physics" and "Kanbun." If anyone remembers them, it's a physics researcher or a Chinese teacher. Because they use it daily for work. Therefore, I guess you can't master anything just by studying at school sometimes.I have never been a good amateur to play. People who perform well are usually professional. That's why you need to be a professional to perform well. **I think what I said brutally honest.**The first is that you take a live admission, play and watch. I think both colleges and jazz schools pay for their studies, but on the other hand, if you get paid and learn, you will improve faster.

***There is no fixed value.**

 Often singing and playing wind instruments will emphasize the importance of abdominal breathing. But if you concentrate on your stomach and inflate or shrink your stomach, isn't it possible for you to go wrong? Where are you breathing in the first place? When asked, wouldn't most people answer three things, "lung", "mouth", "nose"? But that answer is not enough. The answer is, "I have pores all over my body and breathe all over my body." In other words, "the whole earth is breathing" and "the whole universe is breathing". The earth and the universe would be a fictional world, but in short, what you want to say is that people use words to "differentiate" and "segregate" things, create frames and boundaries, and stick to them. You do it. When we say "mountain", we will imagine a mountain like Mt.Fuji, but the mountain is not an independent entity, and it is formed by various things such as "tree", "stone", "sand" That is, the word "mountain" is merely a temporary fixed system called the "mountain", which is separated verbally. As Zen teaches, "words are just fingers pointing to the moon."

For example, in order to show the value of jazz textbooks, they need to be positioned at a larger scale, or music, than jazz textbooks. "Society" needs to be positioned with a measure of "history". As a result of seeking the border of such a larger rule, a border that values everything is needed, and it can be called the "world", but there is no longer a value standard that can evaluate the "world" It does not exist anywhere. So being able to perform well in "dominant motion" is admirable, but it's important to keep in mind that it's just that it shares the system, is worth it in the frame and in the boundaries.

Authors (Akira Kawai, Koji Kawai)

Akira Kawa is An interdisciplinary art researcher and editor

Koji Kawai is a sound artist. He participated in collective improvisation group GAP and he acts with
the unit based on Indian music with Seiji Nagai who was a menber of Taji Mahal Travellers. Now Focusing
on sound, he uses various media, such as an image and molding, and is active in the fields of performance,
art works and research. His works was selected in Santa Fe International Festival of Electroacoustic Music,
ISEA(Inter-Society for Electronic Arts),ISCM(World New music Days) 2010 etc.